Aphelion

First Edition

ISBN: 979-8-9940384-0-6

Library of Congress Control Number:
2025925042

Cover and astrophotography by Daniel Stern
Interior design by Daniel Stern

Published by MEA Observatory Press
Printed in the United States of America

For Mitchell —

whose absence became the spark,
whose silence taught me to speak.

2 Author’s Note

The making of this book began in loss, but what followed was not an act of mourning — it was a search for meaning at the edge of understanding. For most of my life, I lived in the language of reason: numbers, formulas, and the precision of engineering. Astronomy and astrophotography seemed a natural extension of that world — ordered, measurable, and governed by laws that did not waver. Through long nights with my telescopes, I gathered light from distant places, translating data into astrophotographs. Yet, for all its precision, that discipline could not account for what moves within us — what remains when order fails.

Then, unexpectedly, language broke through in another form. Poetry arrived not as craft or calculation, but as necessity — a different kind of observation and means of expression. Where my telescopes gathered light, the poems gathered shadow. They became a voice to answer questions I could not otherwise speak, to reach for truths that resisted equations and diagrams. This collection moves between those two modes of seeing: one scientific, one emotional; one that measures, one that listens. The pairings of poems and astrophotographs are not meant as illustration, but as conversation — between the outer and inner cosmos, between what is known and what is felt. Each speaks in its own grammar of wonder.

The front and back covers mirror this dialogue. Alpha Centauri (front cover), our nearest stellar neighbor, represents proximity — the light we can almost touch. Abell 194 (back cover), a distant cluster of galaxies, 265 million light-years away, bound by invisible gravity, represents what lies far beyond reach. Between them stretches the space the poems inhabit — the aphelion of the human heart, the distance between knowing and feeling, presence and absence, creation and remembrance.

Aphelion takes its name from the point in an orbit farthest from the sun — that moment of separation that still holds connection. These poems are drawn from that distance, from the pull that keeps us moving even as we drift away.

My hope is that *Aphelion* invites you to stand in that space — to look outward and inward at once — and to recognize, perhaps, that what endures is not the flame itself, but the light carried forward.

4

Light travels farther than we can follow.
Still, we look.
This is aphelion —
the distance that still holds us.

Table of Contents

List of Images

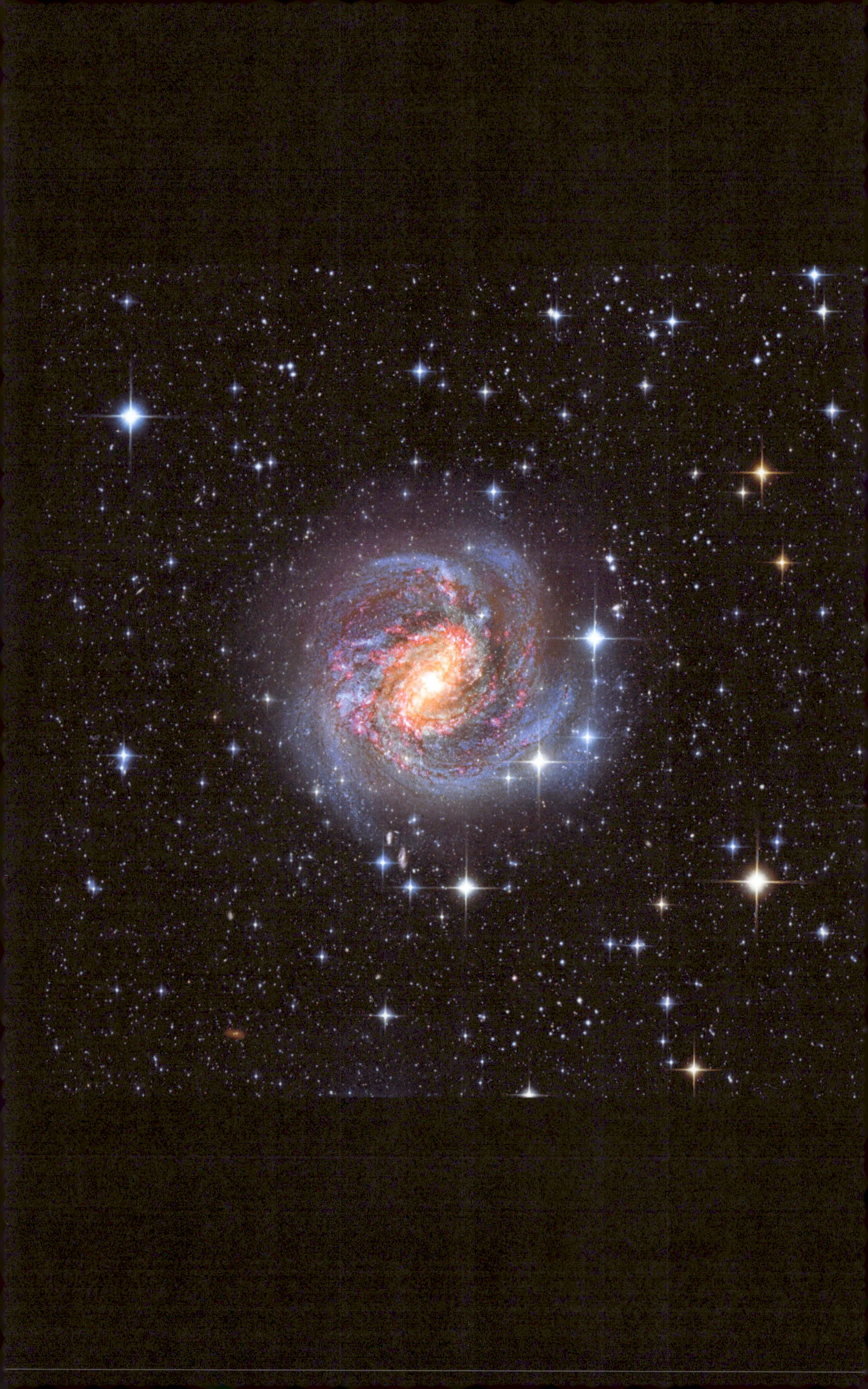

PART I

The Cost of Creation

Art as sacrifice, transformation, and gravity's pull

Messier 83's symmetry hides its history—an unusually high count of supernovae carving brightness into form. It reflects creation not as calm, but as upheaval remade into beauty.

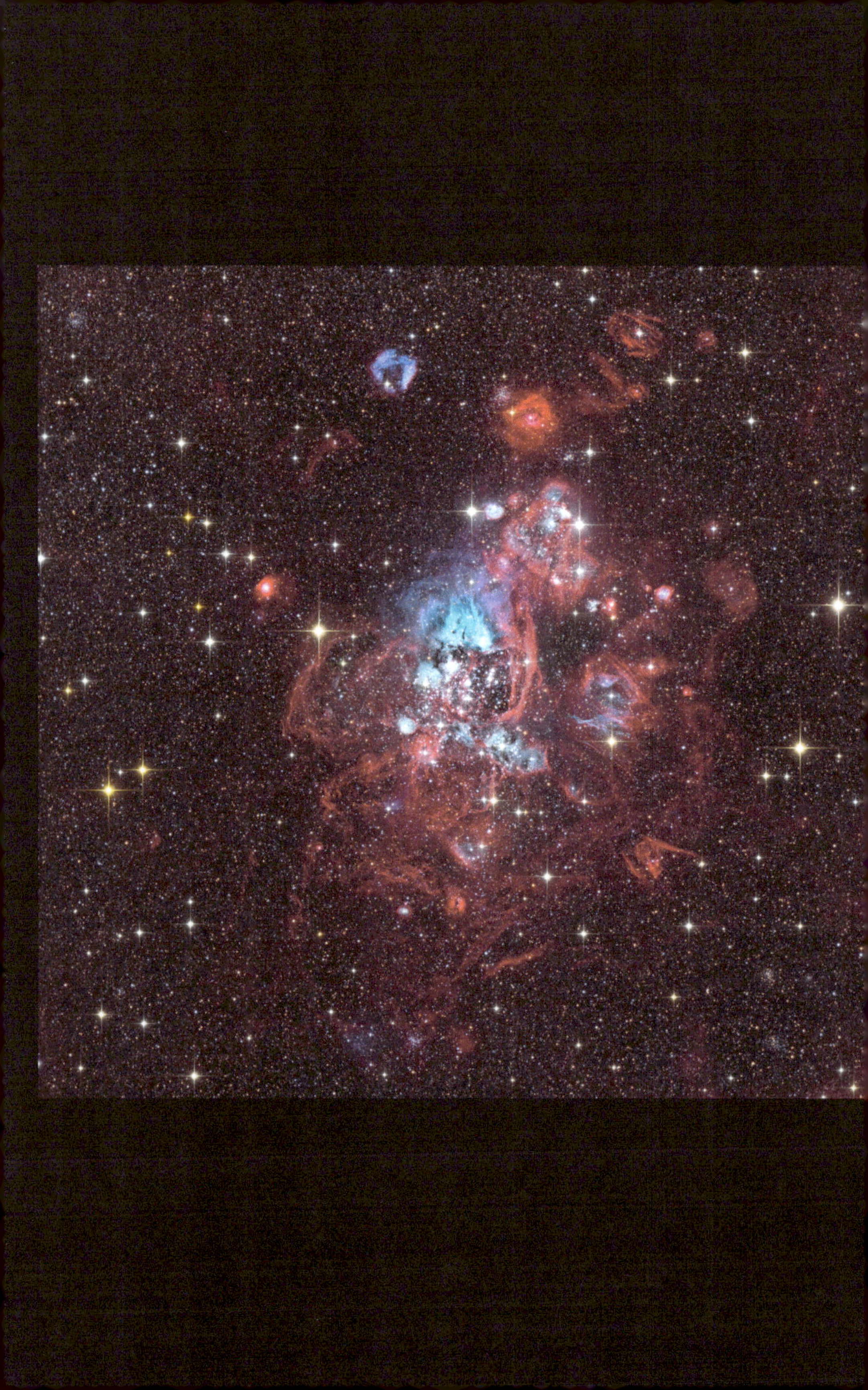

The Price of a Poem

A poem begins in blood.
My son is gone,
yet I write:
each word a slice of myself—
a deliberate sacrifice—
given to the page,
emptiness offered
to the altar of revelation.

A poem begins in silence.
Not absence, but a teacher:
a weight pressing inward,
demanding I face what I would rather bury.
The cost is high:
sleep lost, nerves stripped,
pieces of me gone for good.
Yet in that stillness,
truth speaks clearly.

A poem begins in love.
I remember his birth,
his eyes opening for the first time:
Piercing, limitless depth;
a stare that contained the future.
An olive-skinned vessel lit from within,
held only by time.
That vision did not vanish with his death.
It burns in me still—proof that perfection is real,
even if brief.

The price is always the same:
my safety,
my illusion of wholeness.
Each poem strips these away.
And when I share it,
the gamble deepens.
Sometimes the gift is received,
and I am replenished.
Sometimes it is met with silence—
cutting; cold;
a stinging, wordless verdict.
Even silence is an answer,
and every answer reshapes me.

This meager payment buys me something
I cannot afford otherwise—
a moment of clarity,
a glimpse of meaning,
a fleeting enlightenment
that makes each sacrifice worth it.

So still, I write.
Because through loss,
I learn what cannot be lost.
Because the ruin is also the temple—
every poem, the cost
and the revelation.

"The Price of a Poem" begins in the wound – not metaphorical, but lived, the place where love and loss cohabitate the chest.

N44 is a superbubble formed by repeated eruptions of energy, each burst carving space into light. What appears as open air is the record of violence endured, of stars burning themselves to say something real. The poem makes the same confession: revelation is never free. Each line is paid for in memory, in the risk of being seen, in the cost of telling the truth about grief and love in the same breath. Both nebula and poem understand that creation does not restore what was lost. It illuminates it. The burn remains, radiant and unhidden

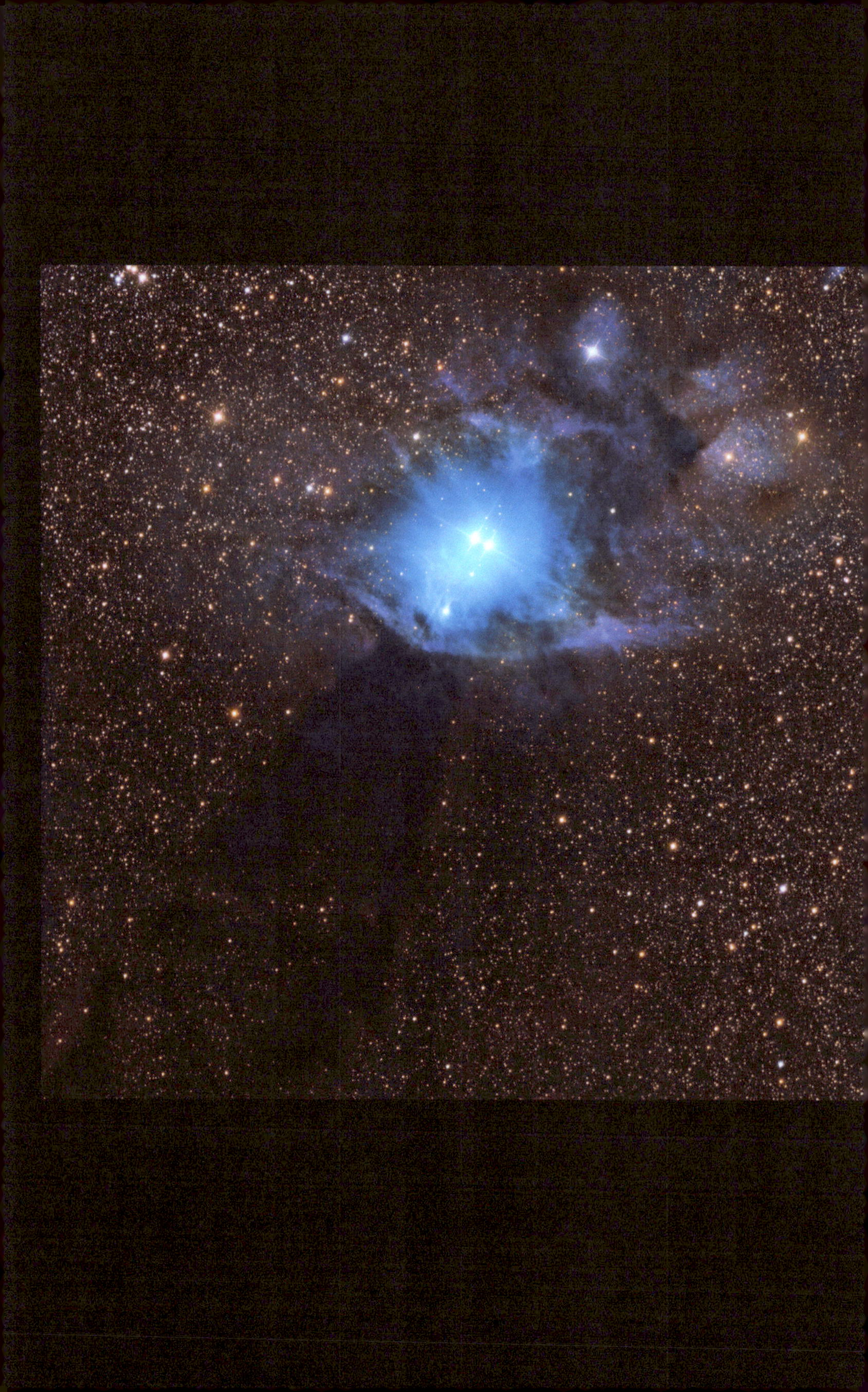

I Have No Skill

I tried a lot of things as a boy.
Not out of passion—
just because adults kept suggesting.

They said try a sport.
So I did—many.
I learned that running hurts
and teamwork is mostly shouting.

They said music builds character.
I learned that character sounds terrible
when it practices,
and the neighbors complain.

They said art teaches patience.
It mostly taught me that fruit sits very still,
and that adults get nervous
when you say you're bored.

They said theater opens the soul.
It opened my soul
and everyone peered in
and nodded with a frown.

After enough of this,
I understood that every activity
comes with someone nearby
ready to supervise my failure.

So I picked poetry.

Silence counts as participation
and missing the point—
is sometimes the point.

There are no wrong angles,
no missed notes,
no coach with a whistle.

No one can tell me I'm doing it wrong.
That's the beauty—
the rules haven't been written.

Or if they have,
I lost them—
on purpose.

Barnard 149 is a dark nebula that hides the stars forming inside it. From the outside it can look empty, but something is developing where we can't see. *I Have No Skill* holds the same idea: doing work without performing it, without comparison or correction. It is not about lacking ability but about having space to grow without being watched.

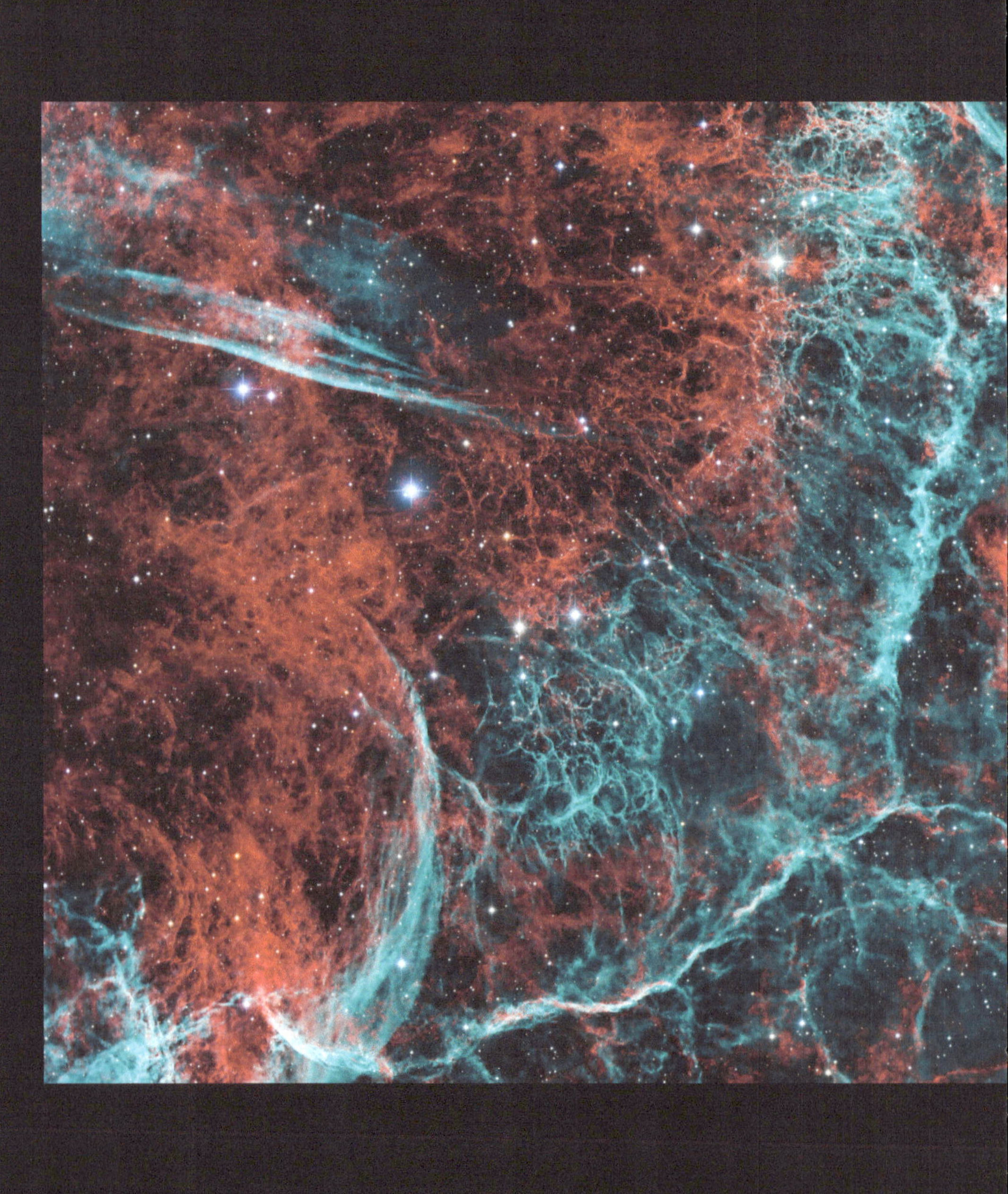

The Furnace Never Cools

Are we not all castings from a mold?
The furnace,
iron poured hot,
cooled too quickly—
but is the shape final?

They called him practical:
his hands carried the weight of noise,
not the drift of words.
No tweed jacket or horn-rimmed glasses,
only an oil-stained blue apron—
clothes that breathed grease and sweat.

Yet in the park,
while his children sifted sand,
he bent over textbooks,
tracing galaxies in unnoticed silence.

Evening settled,
swings stilled,
the constellations quiet—
but he strained to hear their familiar song.

Then grief came.
The ground closed its mouth around a name,
and the mold cracked.
His son was gone.

Nights glowed with memory,
until words rose—
not stammered drafts,
but tempered lines,
iron remembering fire.

They stared, disbelieving.
Because molds, they thought,
were permanent.
Because castings do not sing.

And still, beneath the surface,
we are molten.
Grief softens us,
wonder reshapes,
creation strikes sparks
across even the softest anvil.
Broken iron returns to the fire,
chinks,
burn again.

The mold is never the child,
nor the elder,
nor the silence between.
We are all alloys,
crystals,
waiting for fracture,
for light,
for the hand that remakes.

The furnace never cools.

"The Furnace Never Cools" is about reinvention—how grief remakes rather than ends a life. The Vela Remnant shows the same transformation: a star exploding outward, its debris still glowing as new material gathers around it. What looks like ruin is the start of another structure. The poem stands in that aftershock, learning that endurance is not stoic stillness but the constant reshaping that follows loss.

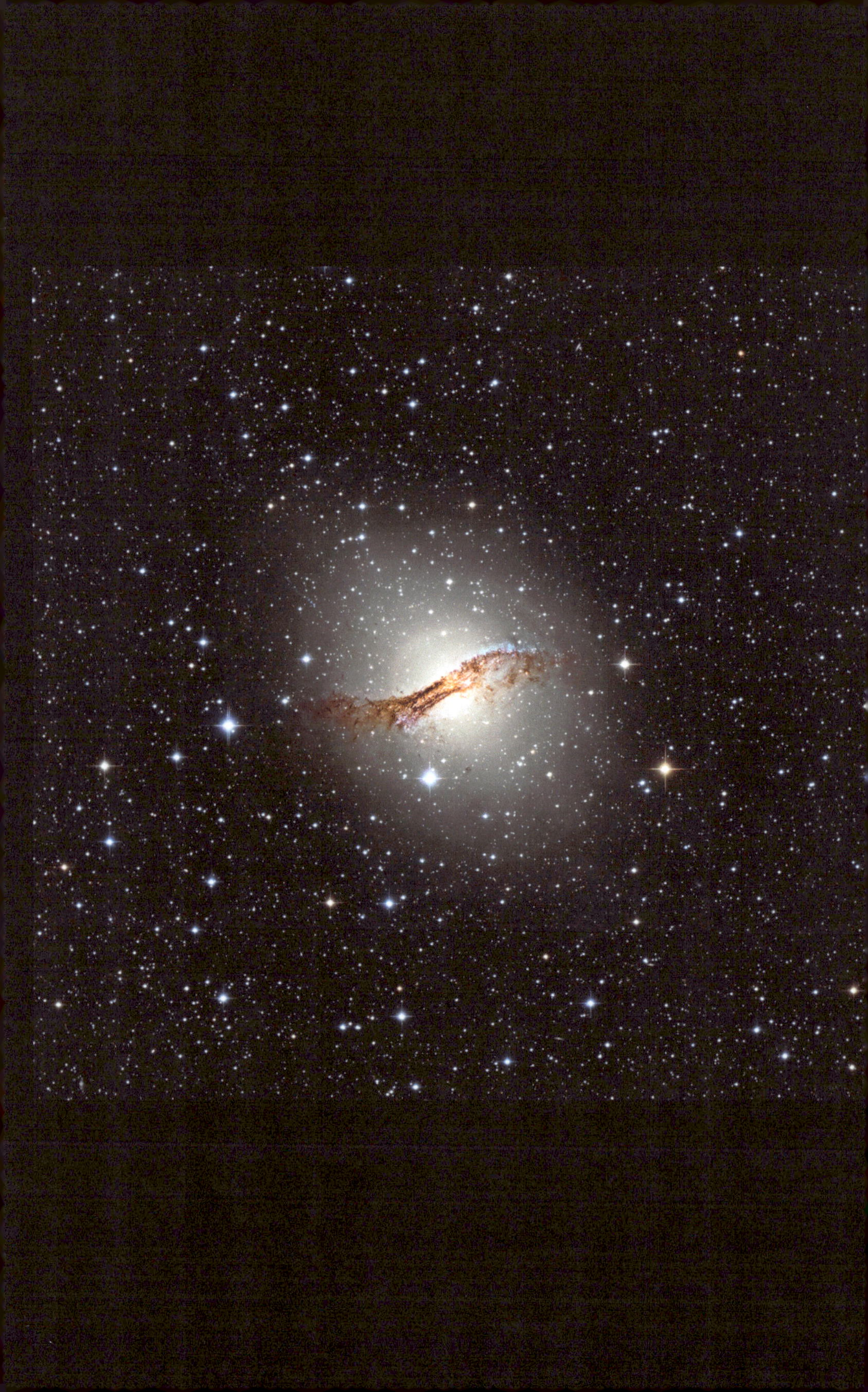

Between Two Gravities

Most mornings,
the sun rises in grayscale,
weighted between two gravities.
I fasten the mask again—
it's thin, too thin—
hoping it veils
what flickers beneath.

I'm tired of being praised for holding it together—
as though silence is sainthood,
as though endurance is free.

I wonder,
if the colors I see
are the same as yours.
Is my red the burn of a star too near,
my blue a trench that swallows light?
Are both tethered by forces I can't unlearn,
by concepts I have no words for?

You see a calm ocean;
I see depths that devour the day.
You feel warmth;
I feel fevered stars
pulling me close
until my marrow softens.

I live in an orbit
that never finds its stillness—
like the mask,
tasting of salt,
sweat dripping down my jaw.

Some days I wonder:
does the mask remember my face?
Does my skin only know
its weight without it?

Between that which demands I shine
and the gravity that pulls me inward,
I keep searching
for a corridor where silence softens,
where wings might hold—
or at least fracture gently
without burning, without breaking.

I smile;
gravity has chosen its pull,
though each curve is a dialect
I'll never master.

You can't hear the fracture,
the pull between quiet and shape.
With colors I no longer trust,
I brace for darkness
behind a brittle smile.

The hues are gone.
Still, the sun will rise in grayscale.
I cinch the mask tighter—
it's easier
to let gravity speak
than ask it to teach you
its language of shadows.

"Between Two Gravities" rests on tension—the pull between composure and collapse. Centaurus A was born when two galaxies collided, their dust and light now locked together in uneasy symmetry. Its beauty comes from that contradiction: order built out of impact. The poem inhabits the same divided space, finding identity not in harmony but in the persistence of opposing forces.

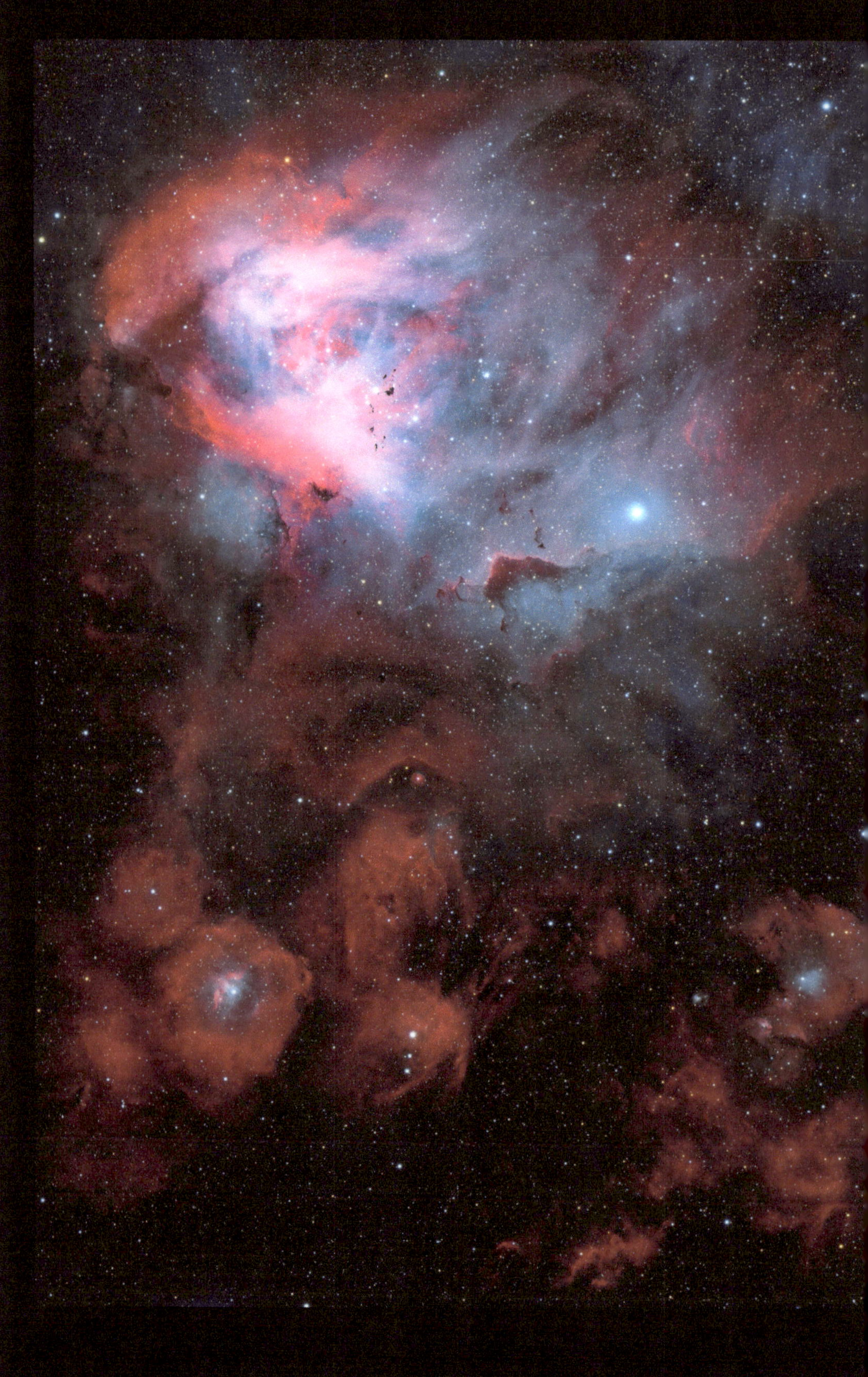

They Teach Me How to Breathe

The desk hums with last night's warmth,
a mug half-cold beside the open book.
They—these pages— live here,
in the stillness between lamp flickers
where paper breathes like skin.

Some curl at the edges, creased
under thumbprints and tears.
Others rest in inked whispers,
their spines remembering every fold,
the faint scent of sleep and stories between them.

They do not need applause.
They need time—
the slow blessing of dust,
heartbeats pressed into margins.

I leave them crumbs of thought,
small crossings-out,
soft words that almost fit.
Outside, a dog barks once—
a single accent too loud for the night.
The fridge clicks,
and the room exhales.

But sometimes they stir before I do,
and I wake afraid they've left me behind.
They teach me to listen
where I once tried to speak.
They rearrange my silence
until I shout their stillness.

By morning, they've outgrown me,
and I ache with pride, with loss.
And I, their quiet author,
breathe beside them,
ink pulsing through my wrist
like something alive.

They Teach Me How to Breathe" speaks to transcendence—the instant when something made becomes its own life. In IC 2944, stars form inside clouds so thick that their first light must push its way out. The poem follows that arc: pages once dependent on the writer begin to move on their own. Both suggest that what's born in darkness eventually finds a way to shine beyond its maker.

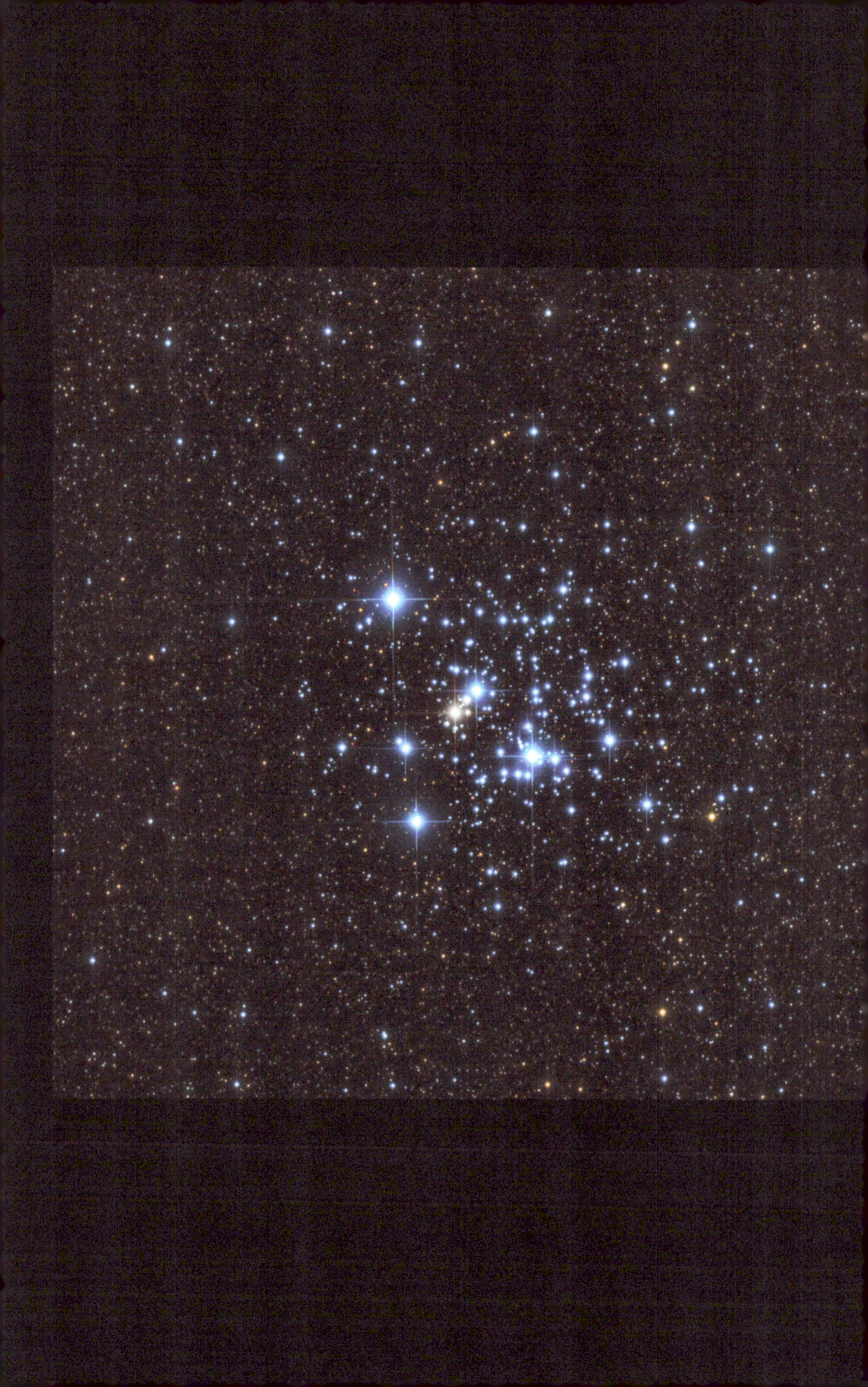

PART II

The Quiet Orbit

Love, inheritance, and the unseen pull of memory

NGC 4755, The Jewel Box Cluster, is a family of stars born from the same cloud, bound not by force but by shared origin. Its bright blues and solitary red giant hold a quiet record of lineage—generations held in a single frame. This section echoes that constellation of inheritance: lives shaped by those who came before, held in orbits we do not choose but continue to carry.

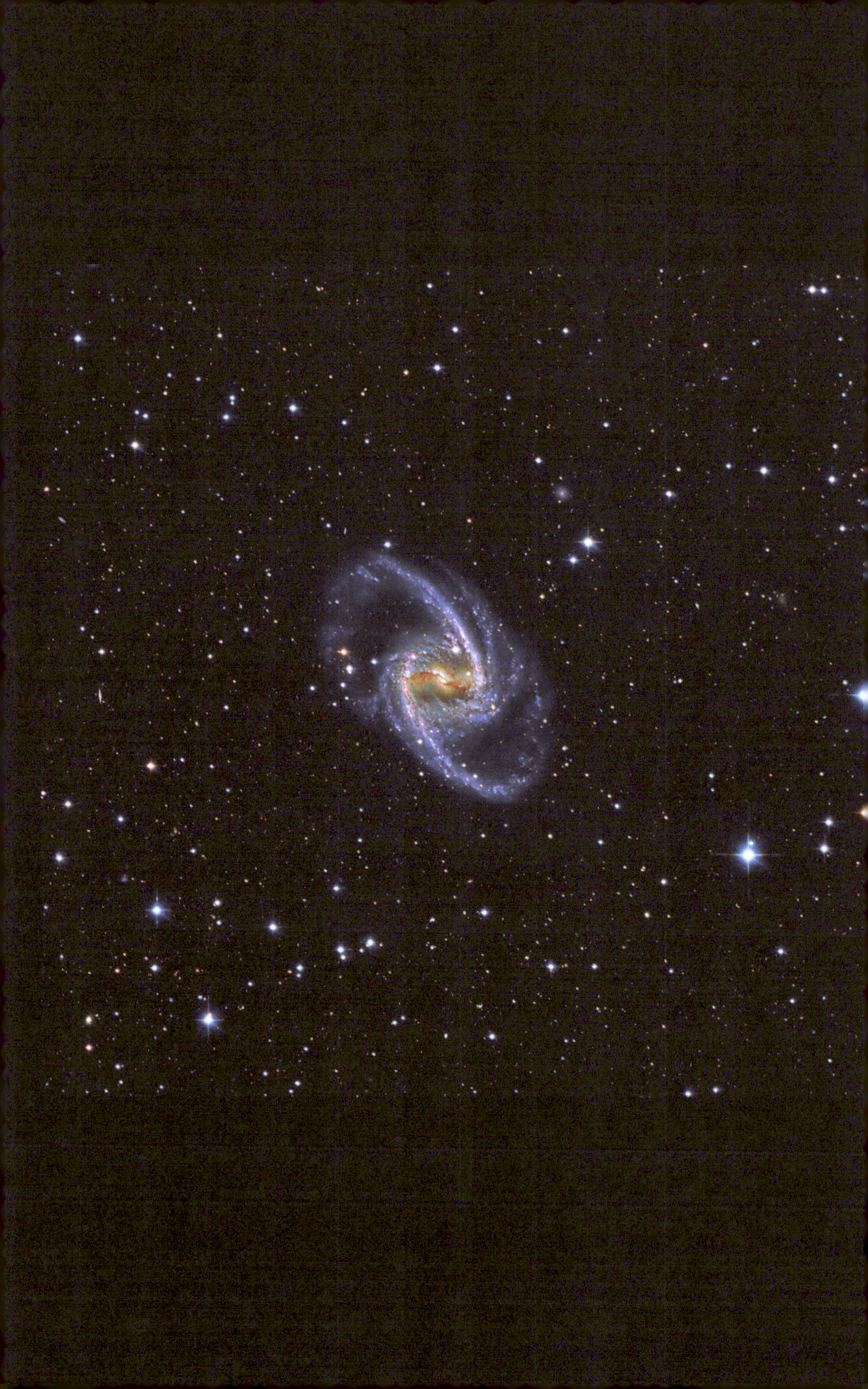

Aphelion - Fathers and Sons

He bore a name I had already mourned,
a sound carried from a time
a force held me too close
to its gravity.

When he arrived, I gave him sky,
wide and unbound,
believing the echo would blaze
a brighter course.

But not every star holds still.
Some slip the constellations we hope to trace,
following a hidden geometry,
their own unseen law.

And when they reach aphelion—
that farthest point
where distance feels eternal—
we feel their silence
more sharply than their light.

Now two horizons pull at me:
one presence too near,
one forever beyond my reach.

They share a name,
yet move in opposing directions,
their orbits carving
the same deep mark.

And I, suspended between them,
cannot tell which absence
defines me more.

Even when the dark grows still,
I look upward,
searching not for light
but for motion—
the slow return
of what seems gone.

For even at aphelion,
a star does not vanish:
it only waits,
just beyond sight,
to draw near again.

"Aphelion – Fathers and Sons" is about memory — not nostalgia, but the living pattern that binds a father I once felt too near and a son now beyond reach. The poem names that split: *two horizons pulling at me... they share a name, yet move in opposing directions;* I wait for *the slow return of what seems gone.* NGC 1365 keeps its spiral even as matter drifts outward, arms curving back toward a persistent center. The image helps see remembrance as a kind of gravity. At aphelion, distance is real, but the orbit is intact.

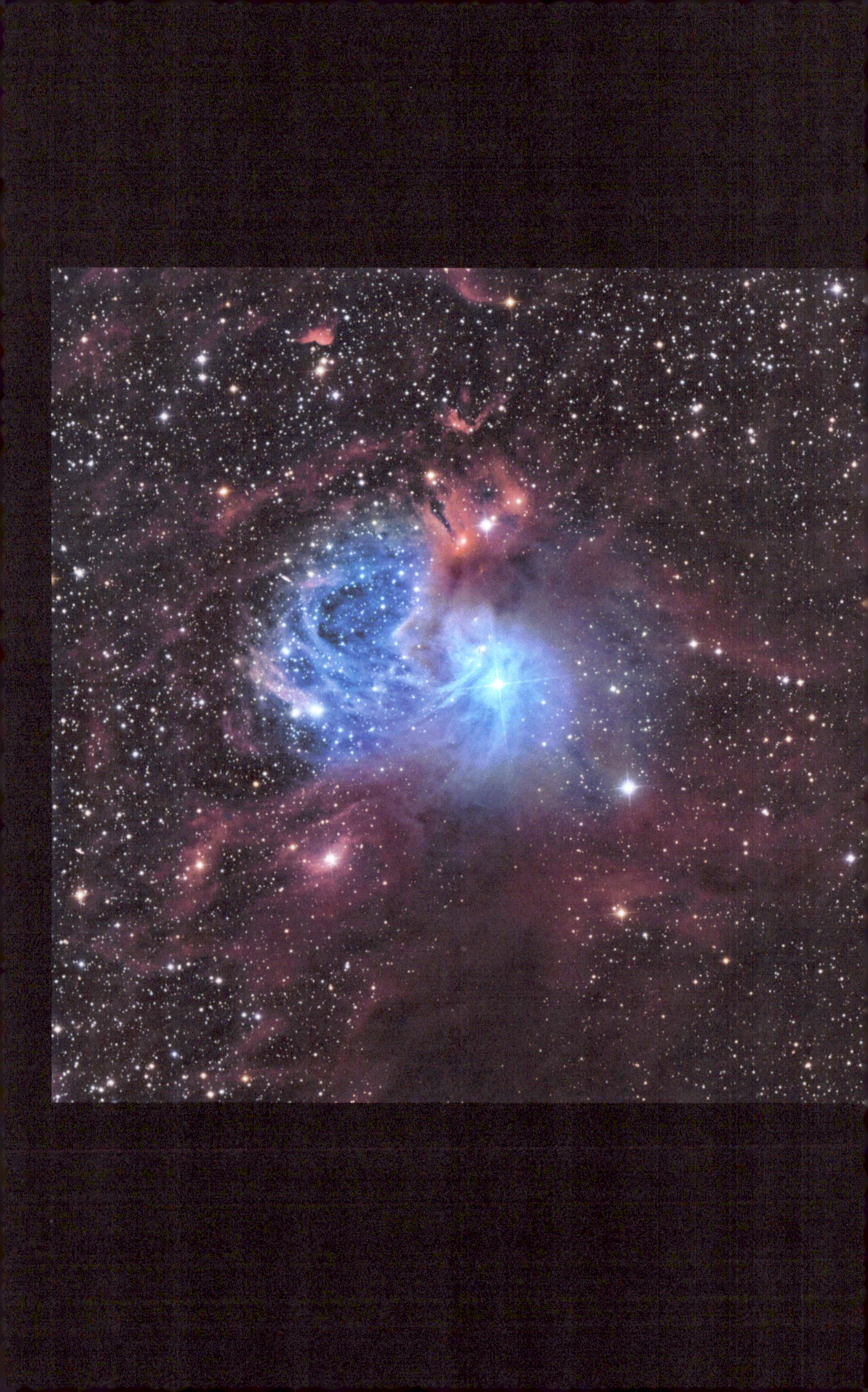

Third Base Theology

The grass was trimmed before I learned to walk,
still wet from some volunteer dad's Saturday morning.
I liked to imagine it waited for me—
as if destiny followed my schedule.

The bat leaned against the fence, casual,
like it recognized me.
I was five.
Everything recognized me.

In the stands, I sat ready for greatness:
the smell of peanuts, a glove broken-in-but-mostly-unused,
my whole body arranged like someone
expecting to be discovered.
Like a talent scout might appear mid–concession line
and say, *Yes.* That one. *The small confused one.*

The dirt knew my name, I said once.
More likely, it knew all names.

The hotdog vendor smiled at me—
not prophetic, just a man familiar
with very confident children.
I took it as fate anyway.

I told myself I was born for this.
This is something children believe
before they learn the idea of "averages."

I tried to make the gift difficult—
stayed late swinging into the dark,
listening to the echo of the ball
I mostly missed.
It was excellent echo practice.

I studied the wind
as if I were preparing to teach a class
on something I barely understood—
nodding at flags, squinting at dust.
No one asked me to do this.

The game didn't answer logic.
(Thank God. I didn't have much.)
It answered timing, patience,
and the ability to style a stumble
as strategy.

I learned from missing—
from balls sailing past while I daydreamed
about how heroic I must look.
Failure was my first language,
spoken fluently.

The bat learned the weight of my hands.
I learned the flavor of infield dirt.
We grew together.

And now, when I run,
I still feel those earlier versions of me—
the ones who thought winning was the point—
breathing behind my ribs.

The wind still sometimes favors me,
or maybe I lean unconsciously toward the path
I've already chosen.
Hard to say which.

Home, I learned, is not arrival.
It's the breath you take
when you realize you're still running—
that running is the point,
and you keep choosing to try
long after the shouting has stopped.

All I own of any of this
is the motion.

And the story I tell of it—
slightly truer each year.

IC 2631 is a reflection nebula. It shines because of the light of a nearby star, not its own. From a distance, it looks self-luminous, as though it created its brightness. But what we're seeing is light it was born into.

Third Base Theology is about recognizing that same situation in a human life — standing in a place prepared before you arrived, praised for effort you didn't have to begin. The poem is the process of noticing this, then choosing to define yourself by what you continue to do, not by what was handed to you.

The light is real.
But where it comes from matters.

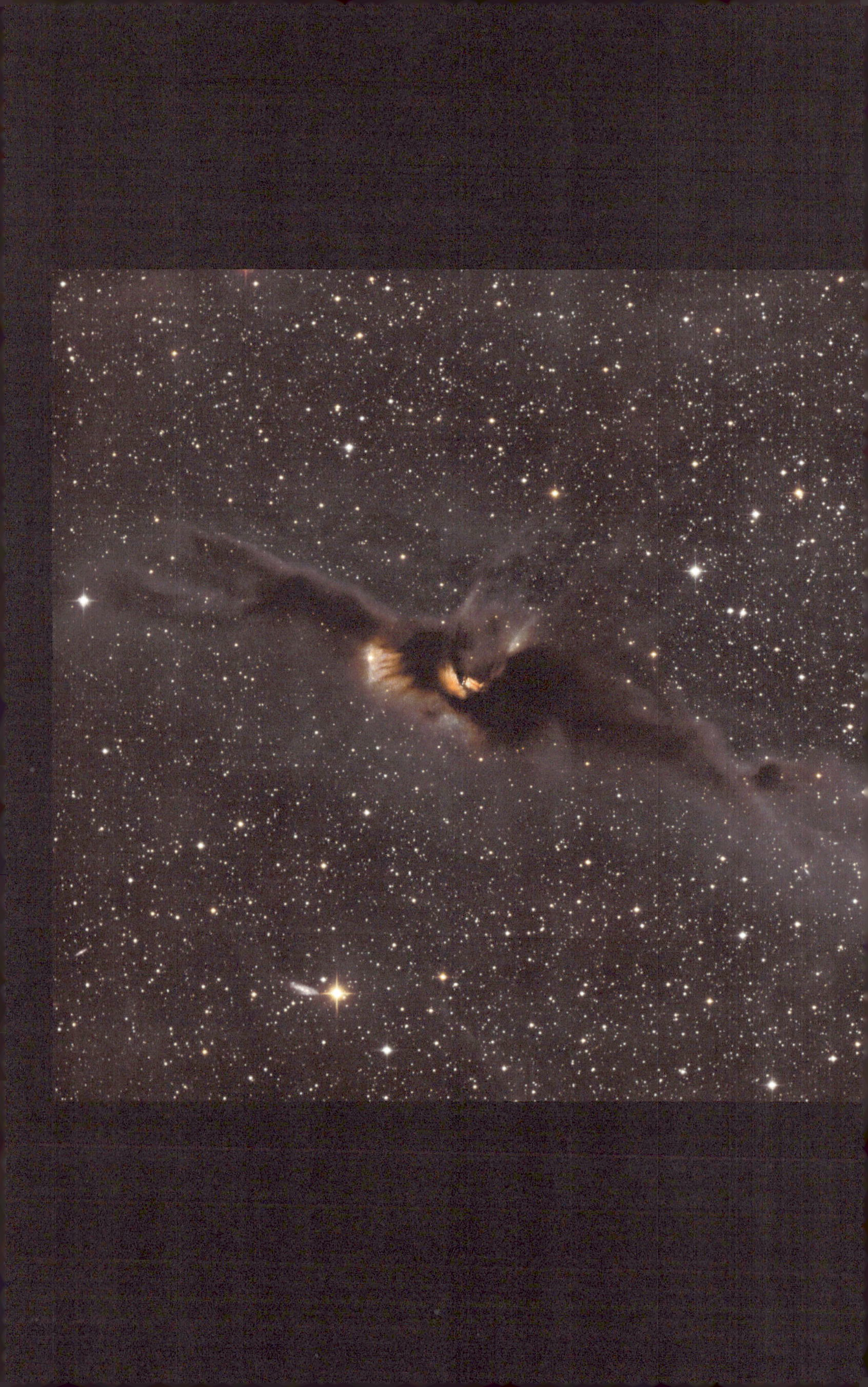

The Quiet Inheritance

He moved like a hidden channel beneath the surface—
finding the difficult path only water learns,
pressing through stone in the dark,
turning aside from the easy light.

I was five when it broke,
but not before it carved its course in me.
Open dreams—
the unlit lantern, waiting.

We lay shoulder to shoulder in the park,
our silence immersed in the stars,
my father's hand tracing constellations,
the sky itself ours to read.

In the kitchen,
he showed me how onions soften in a pan,
how garlic wakes the air,
how laughter can rise like steam.

At the base of the runway,
we sat on the hood of the car,
the air shaking, smelling of jet fuel,
dreaming of destinations.
The roar: a question
we might one day answer.

By the river,
I pointed at the big red ship and said it had candy inside.
The gray one rumbled so hard I covered my ears.
Dad told me its name, but I forgot—
I only remember thinking it looked like a house floating away.
We guessed where each ship was bound,
places in our dreams
just beyond our reach.

In my room,
we spun the globe,
my finger landing at random on a blue one—
Canada, he said,
a place, a story,
the world widening.

Across a chessboard,
he leaned close, whispering moves—
patience in pawns,
the knight's leap,
lessons I only half-understood,
still unfolding in me.

Now the water he carried
spills outward through me.
His inheritance not weight, just motion—
a thirst for knowledge, open books scattered,
a boisterous laugh,
an echo that refused to fade—
a restlessness that looked past fences,
a flame that asks always,
what might be next?

And though his channel ended early,
I walk with its echo in my pulse,
a gift, a burden—
every step a continuation
of the current he began.

“*The Quiet Inheritance*” turns on inheritance — what passes between generations without needing to be spoken. LDN 43 is a dark nebula, its newborn stars still veiled inside the dust that made them. The poem’s daughter receives a similar unseen gift — one that will take time to recognize, its meaning revealed only in her own seasons of light and shadow. Both nebula and poem suggest that what’s most enduring is often invisible at first, waiting quietly to be understood.

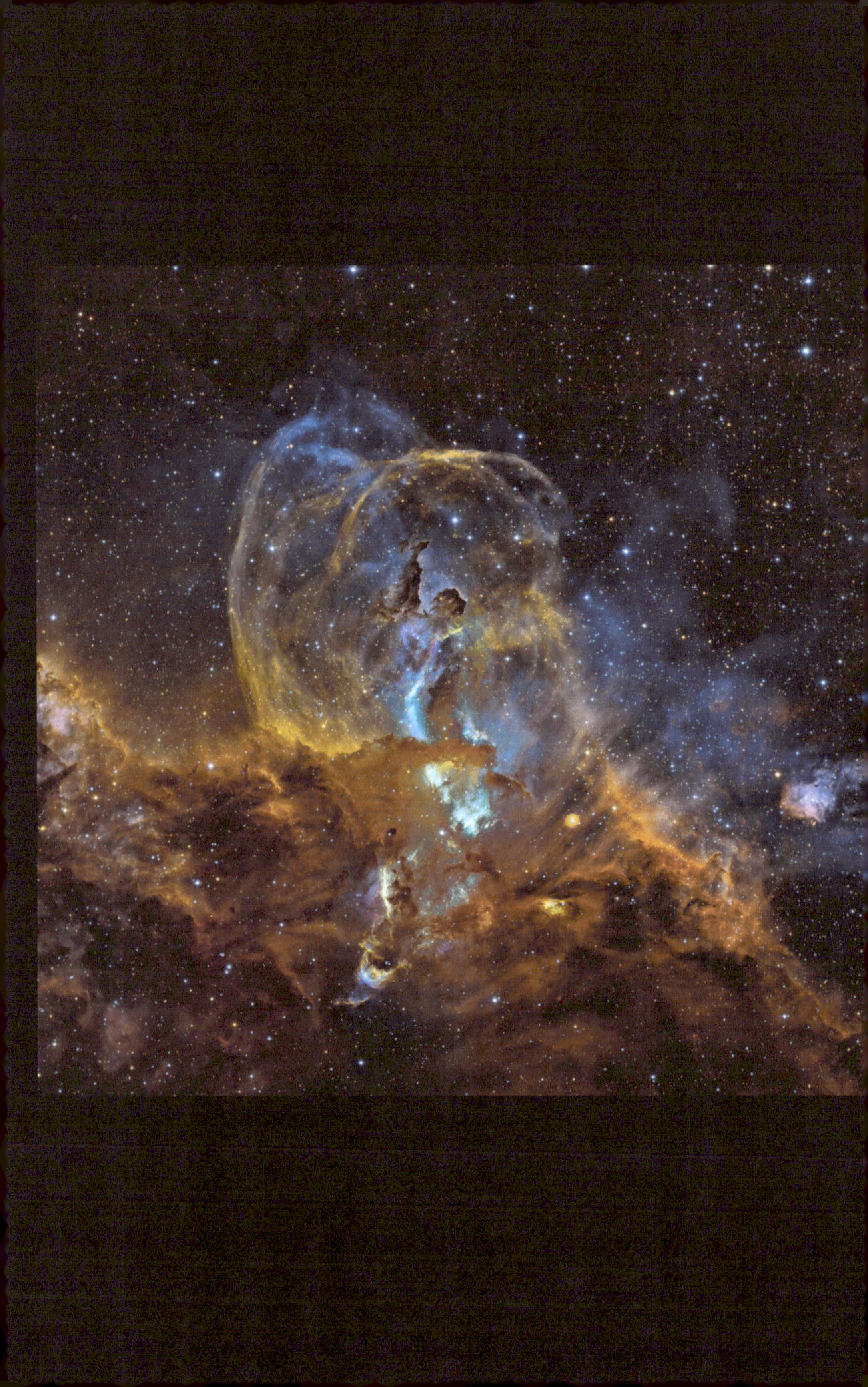

In The Shadow of Giants

Success is not a solitary flame,
but a fire fed by many oils.
We walk among the bones of titans,
their voices strong but far away,
a chorus older than memory
singing the songs of the past.

We do not inherit in fragments,
but in foundations
laid by hands before our own.
But to follow too faithfully
is to forget
that the path forward
must be carved in fresh stone.

So it was with the titans.
So it is with my father.
He left no compass,
only half-remembered deeds.
I chased his memory,
but only later learned:
mirrors distort reality—
and no soul can subsist on shadows alone.

But sometimes I wonder:
had his steps not broken early,
would the shadow of the giants
have been hidden from me?
Would I still have carved a path in stone,
or only traced the grooves of his hands?
The road would be softer,
but not my own.

So I gathered stones—
my palms roughened,
my skin bloodied by risk—
to find that luck is no oracle,
but the child of relentless toil.
The harder the hands,
the kinder Fortune pretends to be.

Fear whispered failure.
I weathered each storm
and leaned harder into the wind.
Every stumble a teacher;
every scar, a memory.

And when I thought the prize was near,
I turned and saw the titans behind me.
Their shadows stretched across my path,
but I bore their weight with reverence—
the bedrock of my achievement.

So I bow, not in triumph,
but in humility.
For in success, as in failure,
the lesson is the same:
We are not monuments of stone,
but apprentices of becoming,
pouring what we've gathered
into hands not our own—
no longer at erosion's mercy.

"In the Shadow of Giants" is about humility — the awareness that what we build begins on ground already shaped by others. The Statue of Liberty Nebula, NGC 3576, is a region of fierce activity: radiation and stellar winds from massive young stars that carve its arcs and hollows, sculpting new structures from the remnants of earlier ones. The poem stands within that kind of inheritance, recognizing that growth depends on groundwork laid before it. Humility here is simply perspective — knowing that creation continues inside the space someone else first cleared.

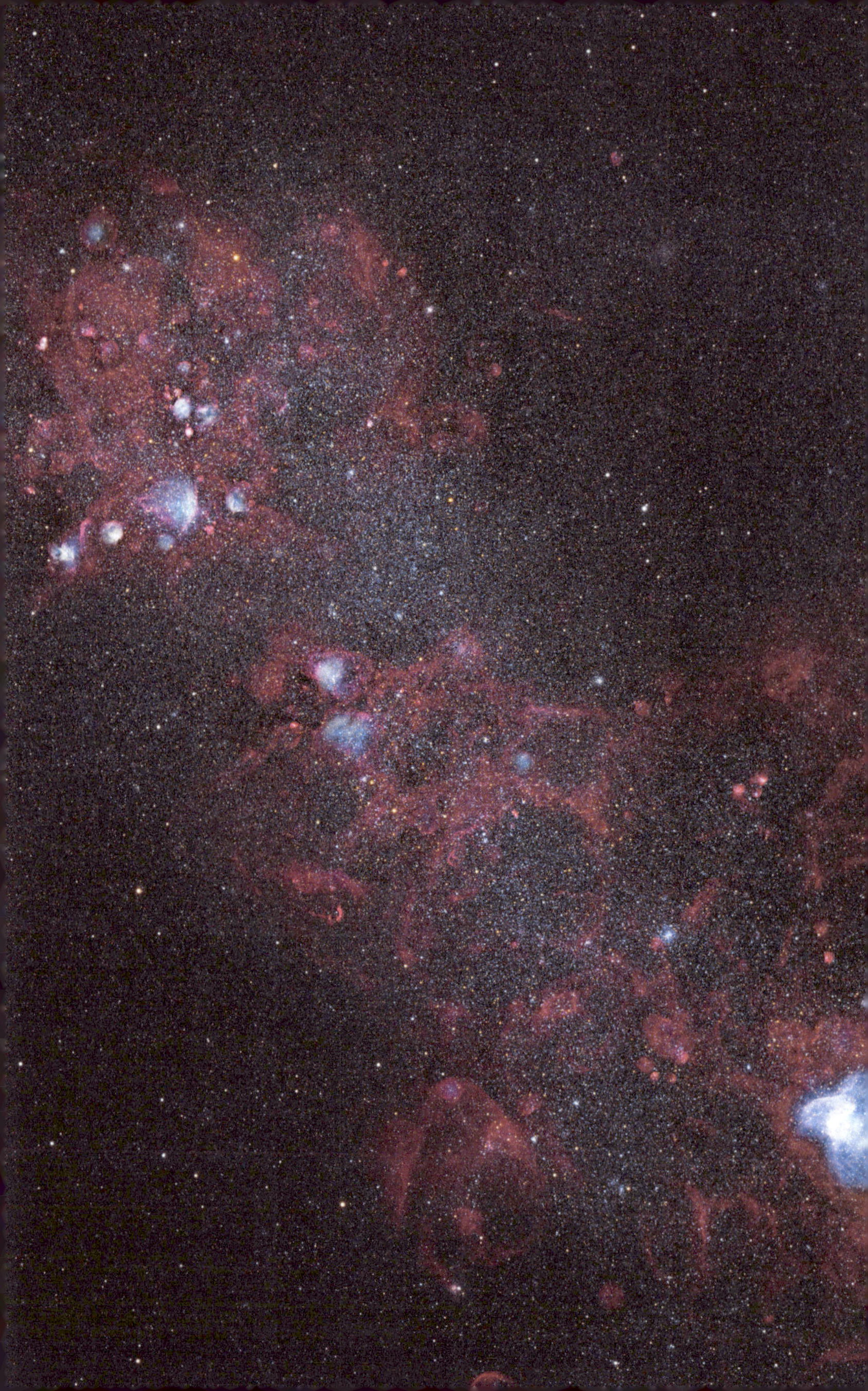

The Lottery Ticket

A paper whisper,
singing numbers not yet seen,
slipped between milk and bills.

I said, *keep it*—
half a laugh, half a prayer.
From the wreck of a still-smoking heart,
six questioning hands
sifting its ash
for proof that something once lived there.

She read the numbers.
Something matched—
not ink,
but the air.
After laughter breaks, a tremor returns
to what was once too quiet to hold.

We laughed at our luck—
not coins, but mornings:
steam trembling from chipped mugs,
a clock coughing toward payday,
small healings
made without words.

Years kept calling their numbers—
work,
laughter,
living,
children learning the shape
of the world.

And her—
not mother,
but quiet laughter folded into care—
a love that never asked for thanks,
but left its fingerprints everywhere.

Then winter came—
white-mouthed,
the kind that stills even the sparrows.

Her breath caught—
light thinned to a thread
through frost in her chest.

I learned the language of waiting—
counting pills;
folding blankets;
measuring hope
the way we once measured luck;
telling myself compassion keeps a list,
though I never saw it.

There were nights
I spoke to no one,
listening for the faint click,
as if the air itself
was learning patience.

And when the thaw came—
soft as light relearning its way—
she opened her eyes,
and the room exhaled into spring.
For a time, the house remembered laughter
bright enough to see by.

But later,
six hands became four.
Two fell silent.

The world grew smaller,
but no quieter.
When the house darkened,
when even the clocks refused to count,
it was her hands
that found the shape of my face again,
her voice steadying the air
I could not fill.

She held me the way
I once held her—
without question,
as if compassion were a baton
passed in the dark.

I hated the weight of being held,
yet stayed there, breathing.

We still buy milk,
still check the numbers—
though never out loud.
Some luck hums anyway,
low and faithful,
under the ordinary sounds of living.

"The Lottery Ticket" is about love and devotion — and how they last through the unremarkable days. The Small Magellanic Cloud, a small companion to our galaxy, keeps its place through mutual gravity, exchanging gas and stars with the Milky Way across long spans of time. The poem reflects that same quiet dependence: two lives linked by routine, by care taken when no one is watching. Love here isn't dramatic or sudden. It's what remains — the shared effort that keeps a world intact.

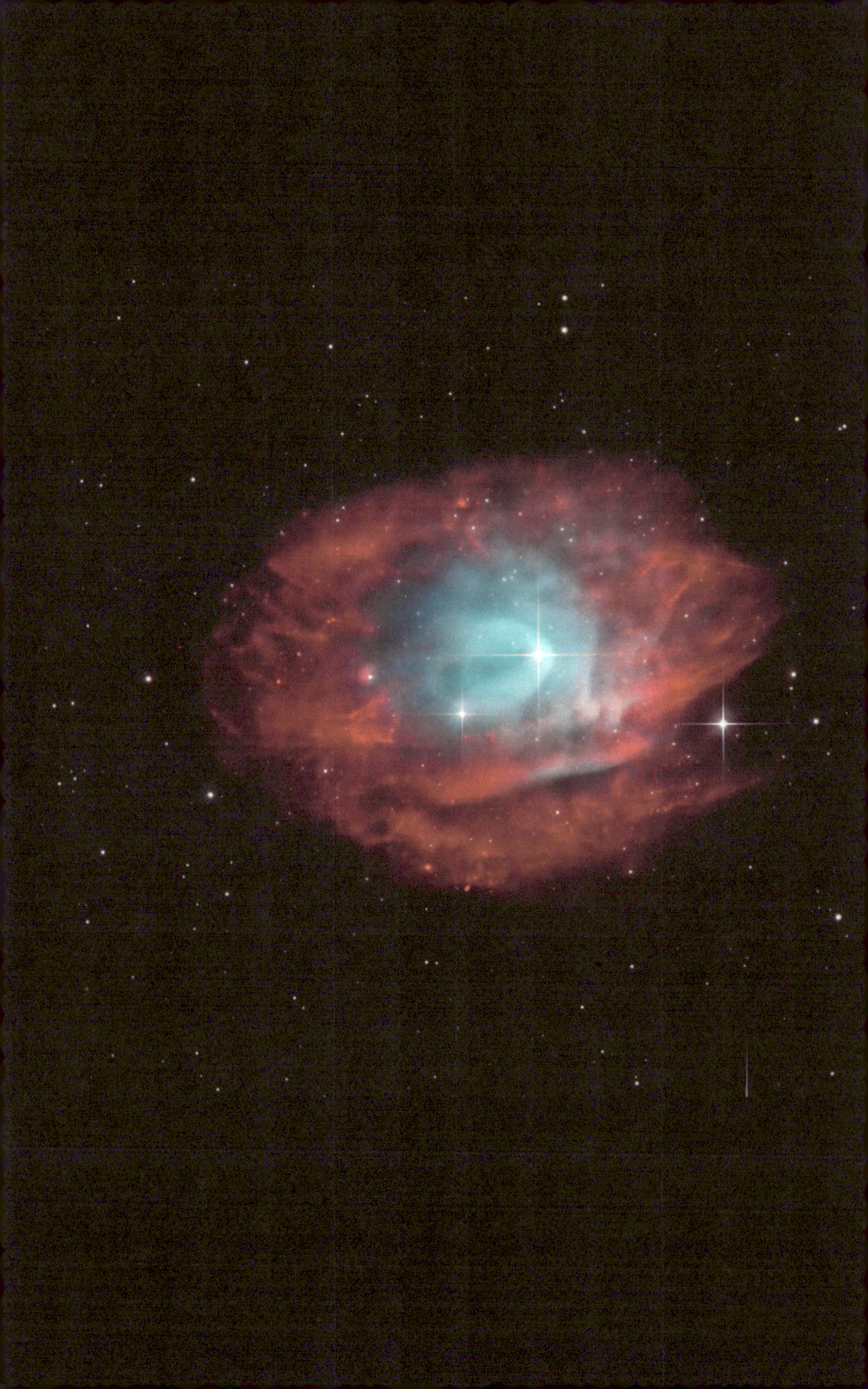

The Buggy Whip Maker

Someone struck stone to stone
and a flame unfolded—
soft as breath,
bright as mischief.

One cave-person shielded their eyes:
"There is too much light.
I can't see the stars."

The stars shrugged.
The fire licked the air.
No apology was given.

A wheel rolled downhill,
all on its own.

The boulder-haulers union complained.

A child watched
and casually invented
faster.

In a village smelling of hay
and the patient judgment of horses,
a man braided leather
into quiet purpose.

His hands: prayer.
His tune: slightly annoying.

A motorcar passed,
coughing,
like a metal animal
learning how to breathe.

He paused,
head tilted slightly—
the universal posture of
What-the-hell-was-that.

A sign changed:

BUGGY WHIPS
(and below, very small)
Consulting - What-the-Hell-Was-That Repair.

The horse retired
to a meadow.
The man learned to listen
to engines—
and go to the bank.
Light rearranged.

Time passes.

A sentence writes itself
only slightly better
than you would have.

You sip coffee.
You squint.
You mutter the ancient refrain:

"...Hmm."

Change is not a storm.
It is a visitor
carrying something wrapped in paper,
tracking dust into your living room,
sitting down in your chair,
waiting for you to notice
you're not the same person
who answered the door.

And we—
we complain
when we can't see the stars,
until we understand
the darkness itself
is part of the light
rearranging us.

Abell 35 is a planetary nebula formed when a star lets go of the material that used to define it. The outer shell is still visible, but the star has already moved on to its next stage. It is a record of change in progress, not of collapse.

The Buggy Whip Maker works the same way.
The poem shows how we outgrow the roles we were sure would last, and how change often arrives quietly—without permission, without ceremony—until we realize we've already become someone new.

What remains is not the loss of what was, but the evidence of having adapted.

PART III

Hunger's Silence

Deprivation, grief, and the long echo of unspoken truth

The Coalsack Nebula is a darkness that defines by withholding—an absence that shapes the light around it. These poems live in that same gravity, where what's missing becomes the story.

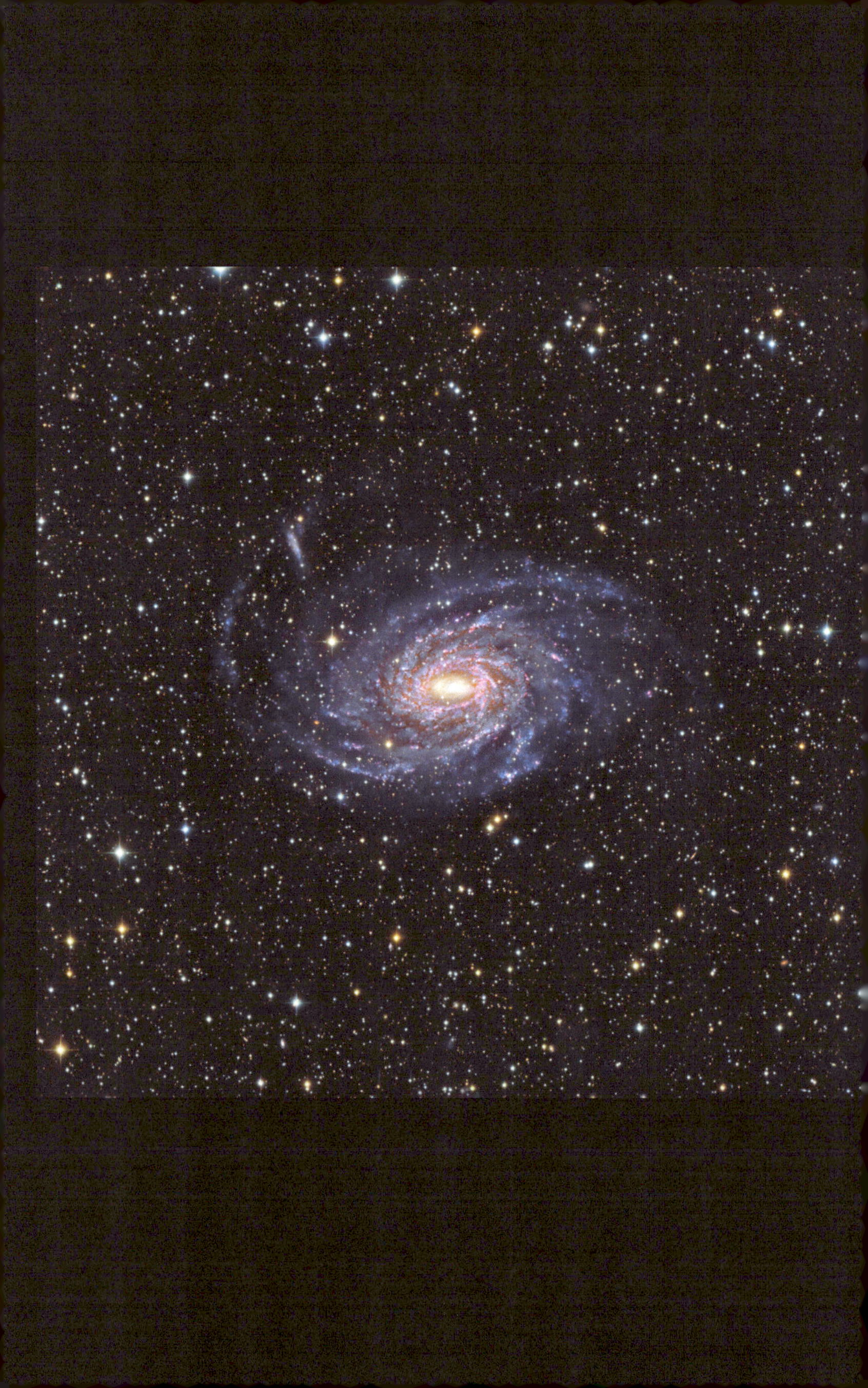

The Starving Feast

They raised a banquet bright with gold;
the tables glittered as though the sun itself was a guest.
But the light felt staged,
a glare meant to blind
those of us who were raised in the cracks
in the floorboards—
we were mice stealing crumbs,
even our shadows unwelcome above.

I reached for the bread—
remembering the rye my grandmother sliced thick,
steam fogging the kitchen window.
This loaf collapsed in my hands;
its crust turned to dust on my tongue
like snow sealing over the mark of a heel,
as if it was never there to begin with.

The wine burned as it passed,
not like the sterling cup
passed down generation to generation,
but like vinegar left too long in the dark.
I swallowed anyway,
pretending it was sweet.

Silver knives rang against plates,
but what landed before us was bone.
Their laughter clanged against my ears—
bells tolling over an altar stripped bare.

I pressed my hunger down—
a sharper ache was elsewhere:
my daughter tugging at my sleeve,
her whisper of *"Daddy, why is my plate empty?"*
I nearly broke then.

My jaw clenched so hard I tasted blood.
I wanted the gold to crack under my fist,
to grind more of their shining bread into dust,
to ask them how it tastes.

I kissed her hair,
my mouth too dry to form the truth.

She asked why the snow forgets her,
why her steps vanish before reaching the door.
I had no answer.
Perhaps snow forgets on purpose.
Perhaps it remembers too much,
closing over us as if we had never passed.

At home, I counted coins on the kitchen table—
three, then two, then none.
Across town their crystal glasses rang;
each toast drove rage's dagger deeper.

I thought of doors closing,
of wages slipping,
of years thinning to days.
And yes, I saw my granddaughter in the frost,
her small hands red from the cold,
her question swallowed before she dared to speak—
a question the snow would bury quickly,
the way it buries every step.

Still, history waits—
though I can't decide if it is patient
or if it simply forgets,
the way snow does.

So I rose from the table,
my chair scraping louder than I meant.
My voice not triumphant, not even whole
but carrying one truth I could not bury:
silence feeds no one.
And if the snow erases my path,
let it do so only after I've spoken.
I will not teach my children hunger quietly.

NGC 6744 is a large spiral galaxy that appears balanced and complete. But part of its structure comes from a smaller companion galaxy being pulled apart. From a distance, the spiral looks graceful. Up close, you can see what it took to make it look that way.

The Starving Feast stands in that recognition. It refuses to call scarcity "tradition," or to teach a child to be grateful for what does not nourish.

The poem names what is missing—and who paid for the appearance of abundance—so the pattern does not continue.

Seeing the cost is the first act of change.
Saying it out loud is the second.

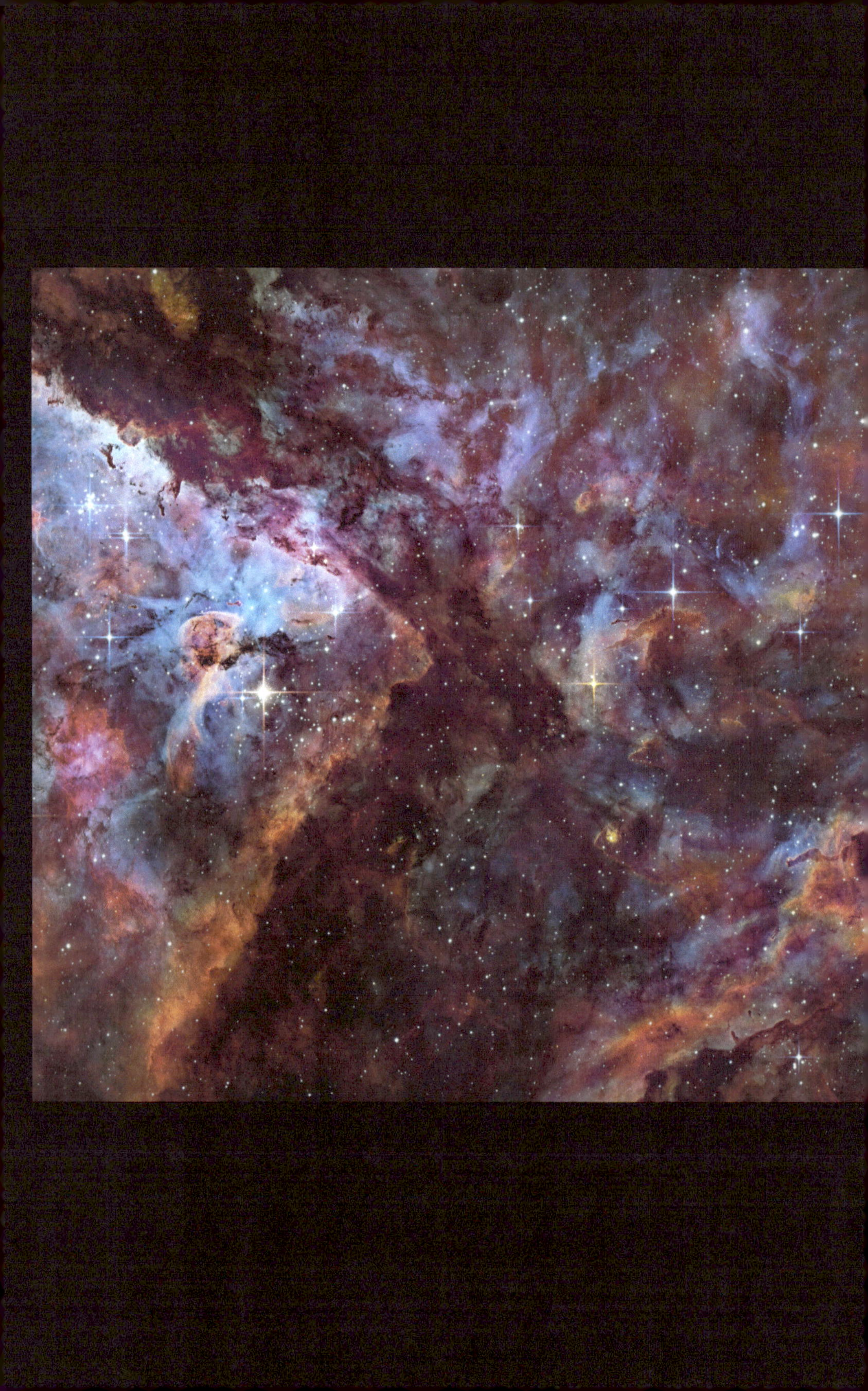

The Roar of Silence

The loudest answer to any question
is silence—

a throatless roar,
an awkward hesitation
between question and reply,
an em dash stretched across air.

Suspense hangs.
Body language screams.
A sign.
A signal.
The sharp scent of disapproval.

And worse:
the response that never comes,
a message left unread,
a question unworthy of reply.

The sting settles in—
what I offered
did not deserve an answer.

******

Silence deepens,
the harbinger of loneliness.

Yet it is also fertile—
a catalyst for inspiration,
moving forward in the dark.
But sometimes,

a stillness mistaken for discovery,
a hush is disguised as revelation.

******

Then the rupture:
A call from a stranger informing me,
my son is dead.

Do not tell me
this is where meaning begins.

Breathing stops.
Blood turns cold.
A dry tear stains my face.

And all I can summon
is silence.

******

Afterward, my memory races
from embarrassment
to shame,
shame to silence again,

the hollow echo shouting louder
than any voice.

******

So silence becomes a cathedral,
vast and unforgiving,
its arches built of absence,
its hymns
having left through open doors.

It is desert and oasis both,
teaching that grief and truth
are carved from the same void.

Silence is what greets me at night—
staring at a shadow,
born of light I cannot see,
the beat of a pulse
waiting, waiting—
the only sound that answers back.

The Carina Nebula is a region of extreme creation and collapse. Massive stars are forming, others are tearing themselves apart, and shockwaves are reshaping the gas around them. From Earth, it looks calm and silent, but its stillness is only distance. Up close, it is one of the most violent places we can see.

The Roar of Silence comes from that same kind of moment — when something shatters, and the body cannot speak around it. The poem stays inside the quiet that follows irreversible change, when meaning is present, overwhelming, and wordless.

Silence here is not the lack of sound.
It is what remains when life has been rearranged
faster than language can catch up.

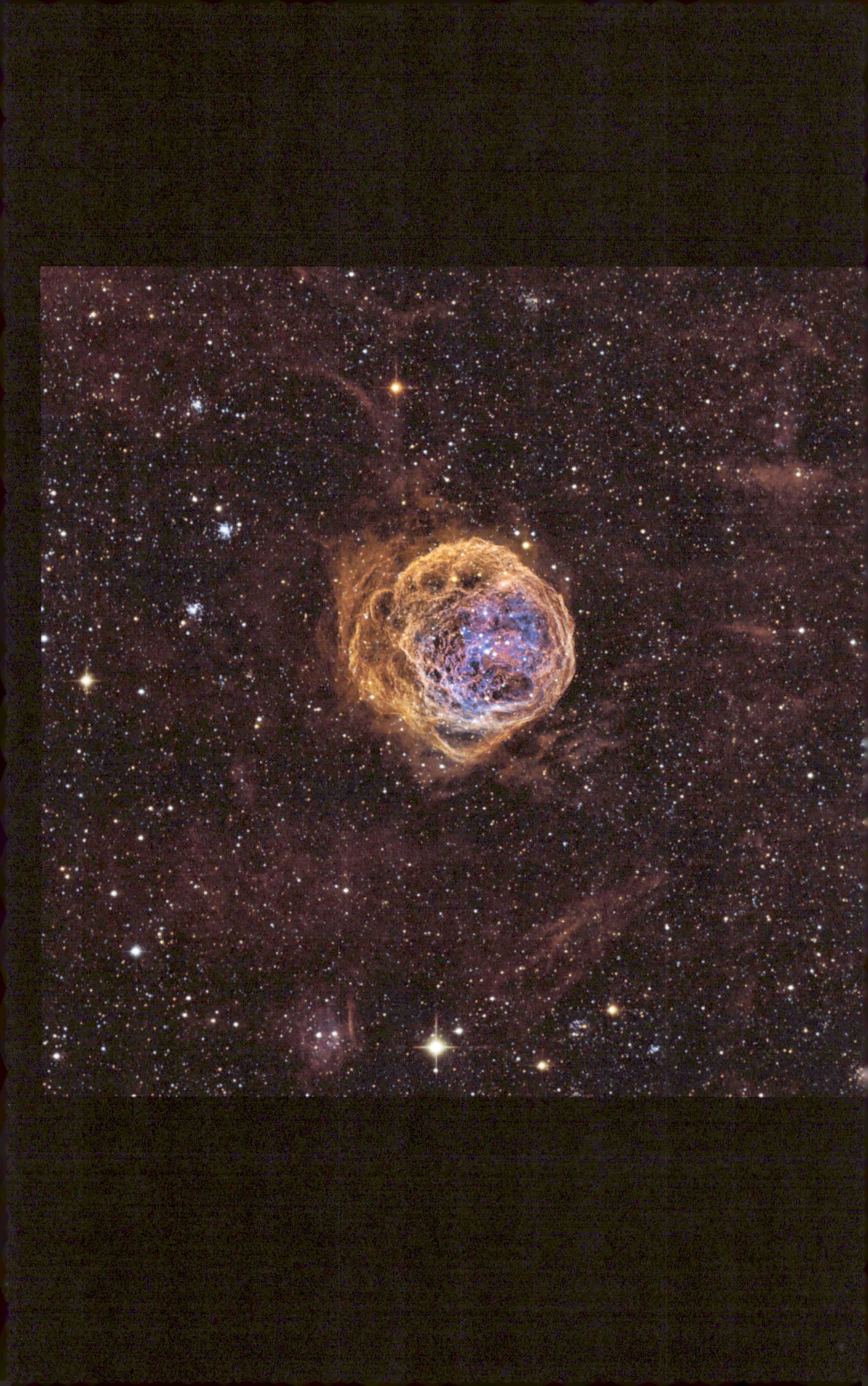

Estate Bottled

They crush their own grapes
under banners of red and blue—
swearing this year,
this harvest,
is different.

They pour the wine in front of cameras,
tilt the glasses to the lights
so the whole country can watch it glow.
Watch it prove them right.

They drink slowly,
as though savoring themselves—
as though the flavor confirms
everything they already believed.

The room hums with self-congratulation.
Their laughter soft and satisfied,
the sound of people convinced
they have done enough.

I watch it—
on a screen glowing too bright
in a room gone quiet.

The anchor's voice is smooth as lacquer,
sliding past stories
that barely register as stories anymore.
The taste of it sits in my teeth. It will not leave.

Outside—
the fields crack.
The rows stand silent.
No workers bending at dawn,
no hands,
no voices—
just wind
dragging dust across abandoned furrows.

People die quietly
in unlit rooms,
in counties that disappeared
from the budget notes,
in waiting lists that never moved.

I don't know their names.
That's the part that hits hardest—
how easily a life becomes
a number,
a headline,
a passing ripple
in the bottom corner of the screen.

But the victors swirl their glasses,
call the flavor "complex,"
"hard-earned,"
"deserved."

They do not taste
the salt at the rim.
They do not notice
how the wine pulls heavy on the tongue,
how it stains deeper each season.

Someone laughs,
calls it the best vintage yet.
Pours another.

They toast themselves
for caring.
They toast themselves
for winning.
They toast themselves
for being the ones
who understand.

The glasses are spotless.
The table is white.
No stain touches the linen.

But the wine—
the wine remembers.

And it is getting harder
not to taste the blood.

"Estate Bottled" watches power toast itself while the cost of its victories is borne elsewhere – unacknowledged, unnamed, ungrieved.

Henize 70 is a superbubble created by many past explosions, their force expanding into one another until the air itself is shaped by what happened long before. The nebula does not erase its origins; it holds them. The poem stands in that same atmosphere. The celebration on the screen is polished, practiced, seamless – while the absence beneath it widens. Both poem and nebula refuse the forgetting. They know that what is harvested has a history. What is raised in a glass has a lineage of labor, of silence, of bodies missing from the table. The wine remembers. So does the sky.

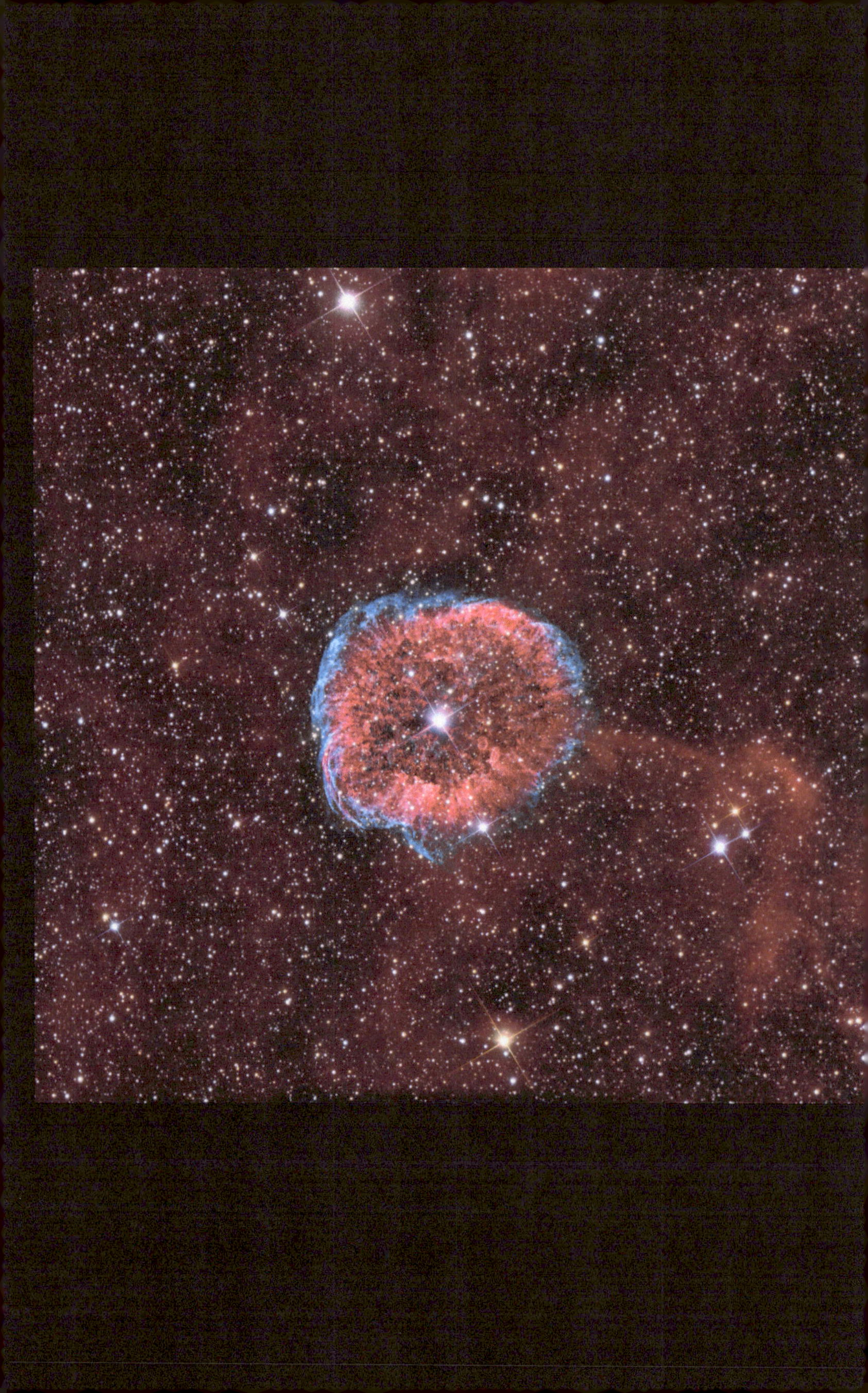

The Unwelcome Ride

The doors gasp open.
The elevator exhales—
lungs of steel breathing out
fear, hope, the faint perfume of antiseptic.

Somewhere in the hospital
babies are born—
but here only gravity cries.

I press the button marked *Up.*
The light answers, steady as a pulse.
And though the ascent is brief,
for a moment,
my shoulders loosen—
grief becomes motion,
not weight.

As I rise,
I wonder which world waits—
her half-smile behind the mask
or a fever packed in ice.

I remember her hair
before room 610 took her name.

Unacquainted friends—
his son, my wife.
A nod, a glance—
our fragile treaty.
Fellow travelers,
each pretending not to drown.

Between stops,
the silence trades faces.
Each floor a decade,
each *ding* a reckoning.
I count the distances grief invents.

There is no sun here—
only the tune of surrender.

The elevator hums again,
its cables trembling.
The whoosh of her room fills my head.
Doors sigh apart, then seal shut—
the sound of going on.

When the door's part again,
the air flinches before I do.
I step out—
not brave,
just faithful.

My shoes whisper across waxed tiles,
careful not to disturb the quiet.
Stale coffee lingers.
The walls remember what I forget:
every rise is matched by a fall,
every breath is a negotiation.

He stands where he always stands—
coffee cooling,
grief hardening in his hands.
We never speak,
but his silence answers mine:
a breath held too long,
two languages speaking the same dialect of fear.

Between breath and step,
the world tilts—
antiseptic fading
to rain.

I let the silence finish speaking.

I step inside again,
doors close softly—
a sigh, not a seal.

Now when the doors open,
the air is light.

Her laughter lingers,
small, certain—
a pulse rediscovered.

The walls hum,
alive with leaving.

The button glows behind me,
constant, forgiving.

And for once,
I do not look back.

"The Unwelcome Ride" is about resilience — the ability to keep moving when there's no choice but forward. RCW 58 formed when a massive star began shedding its outer layers, creating a ring of gas shaped by powerful winds from the unstable star at its center. Even as it loses itself, the core endures and continues to shine. The poem understands that kind of survival — not heroic, just ongoing. Both show that resilience is rarely chosen; it's what remains when everything else has already gone.

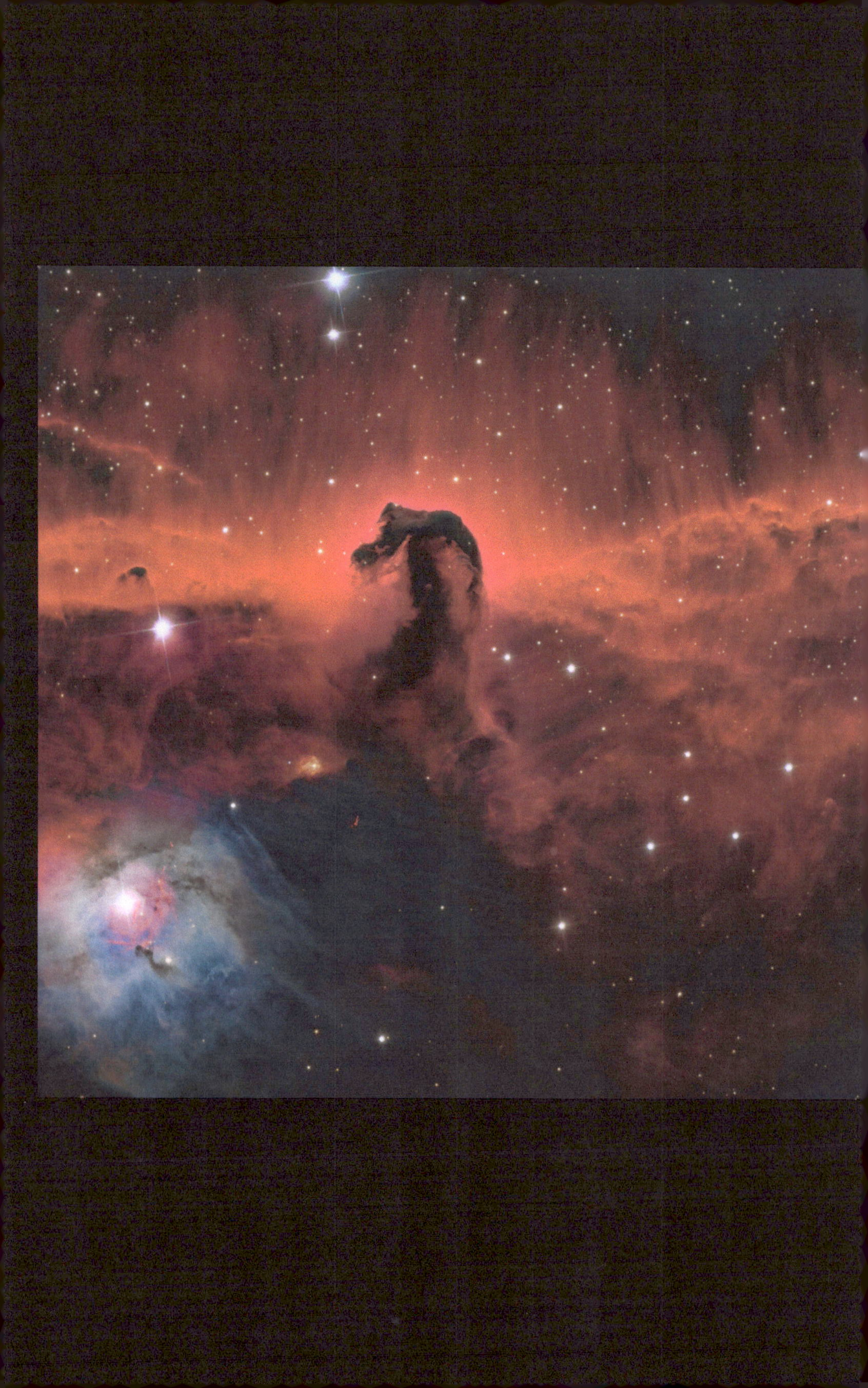

The Neglected Lantern

They gather on the balcony,
torches wavering in the wind—
bright, reliable flames
that shout their importance.

Sparks drift down in small, wandering arcs.
Two children step back at the same time,
their hands finding each other
before any parent thinks to reach.

One man fumbles his torch,
catches his breath too sharply—
a fear the children hear
more clearly than the fire.

Behind the crowd hangs the lantern—
glass dulled,
a thumbprint smudged along the pane,
its wick bent like a question.
It was meant to glow
when the night grew uncertain,
meant to be the quiet kind of guidance
torches never give.
No one looks at it.
No one wonders why it's dark.

A boy lifts his arm, pointing—
a small sleeve slipping down,
a silent question waiting to be answered.
No one notices.
No one speaks.

I remember my grandfather's lantern—
how he lit it with steady hands,
coffee on his breath at dawn,
warming the glass after cold mornings.
Not a tradition, he said,
just a way to help someone home.

But tonight the torches roar,
and still the lantern hangs untouched.
The crowd leans back,
just slightly—
a shift only the children feel,
their fingers tightening around one another.

The sparks keep falling.
The lantern stays dark.
And one by one,
the children stop looking up—
stop waiting for a light
that will not rise—
and begin watching the ground,
learning too early
that vigilance replaces guidance
when no one tends the flame.

The Horsehead Nebula is a darkness made visible—its shape defined not by what it shines, but by what it refuses to let through. A red sheet of hydrogen light (IC 434) burns behind it, bright enough to carve the silhouette that interrupts its glow. The void becomes a figure only because the light around it is relentless. *The Lantern That Refuses to Light* stands in that same tension: a world loud with spectacle, yet absent in guidance; illumination everywhere except where it is needed most. Both poem and image understand that neglect has a shape, that failed responsibility casts a shadow sharper than flame, and that sometimes the darkest part of the sky is the place where a light should have been tended.

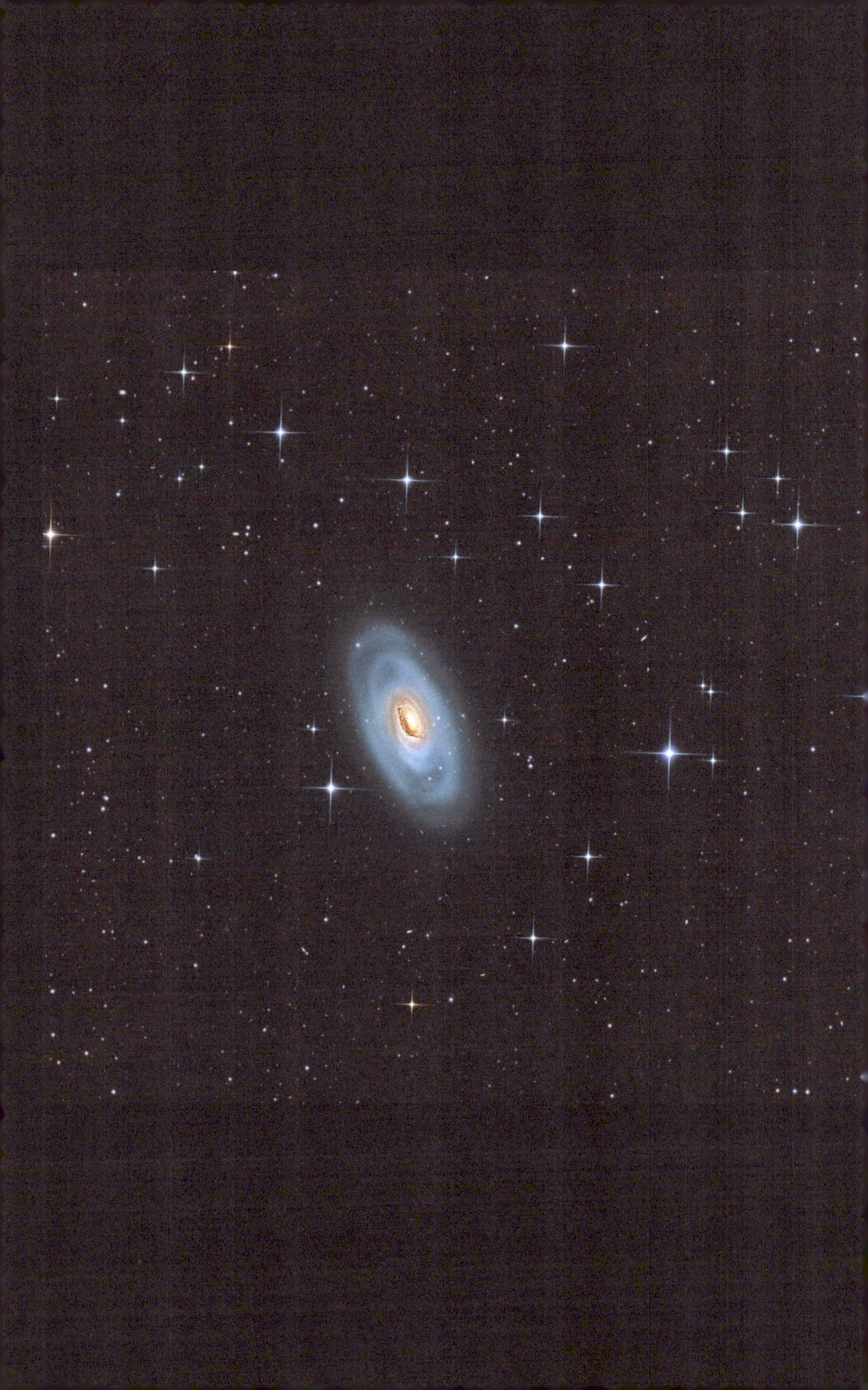

Where are the Children

I was there when the child vanished—
not in hunger's slow dimming,
not in the noise of war,
but in a fevered night
where breath grew thin,
and help was a promise
stalled in a room
of polished tables and dark suits.

Her shoes by the door.
Mosquito net folded neatly.
A cup on the counter,
water still warm.

With the sun overhead,
the nurse asleep on a bench,
only silence filled the cabinet
where the answers once were.

Outside, rain gathered in ruts,
small mirrors for the sky,
a place for wings to grow their armies—
the mud below closing its mouth
around too many names.

At night, I tried not to think
how fast a forehead burns,
how still a chest can become.

I remember the weight of her,
lighter than she had ever been—
fever stealing not breath
but gravity.

Bullets are expensive—
compassion is not.

Someone approved the budget.
Someone signed the order.
Someone slept.

The ledger balanced—
but their signatures outlived
the children they erased.

Years pass.
Faces thin out
from memory first,
then from the photographs.

Sometimes I see them in dreams—
small hands fluttering
like wings against heat,
a kite rising over a field,
the string slipping loose.

The ledgers sleep on shelves.
Dust settles without shame.

History will remember—
not because it grieves,
but because it keeps what is written.

And when it does,
they will not understand.
Someone will ask—
where are the children?

NGC 4826, the Black Eye Galaxy, shows a bright central core crossed by a stark band of dark dust. Part of the galaxy rotates in the opposite direction from the rest, evidence of something absorbed that changed its motion. From a distance it appears intact, but up close you can see where something has been taken in and partly hidden.

Where Are the Children holds the same truth.
The poem remembers what was lost where the record insists on order.
It refuses to let absence become erasure.
The silence, the documentation, the unanswered questions—these do not mean nothing happened.
They mean something happened that must not be covered.

The dark band is not emptiness.
It is what remains of what was taken.

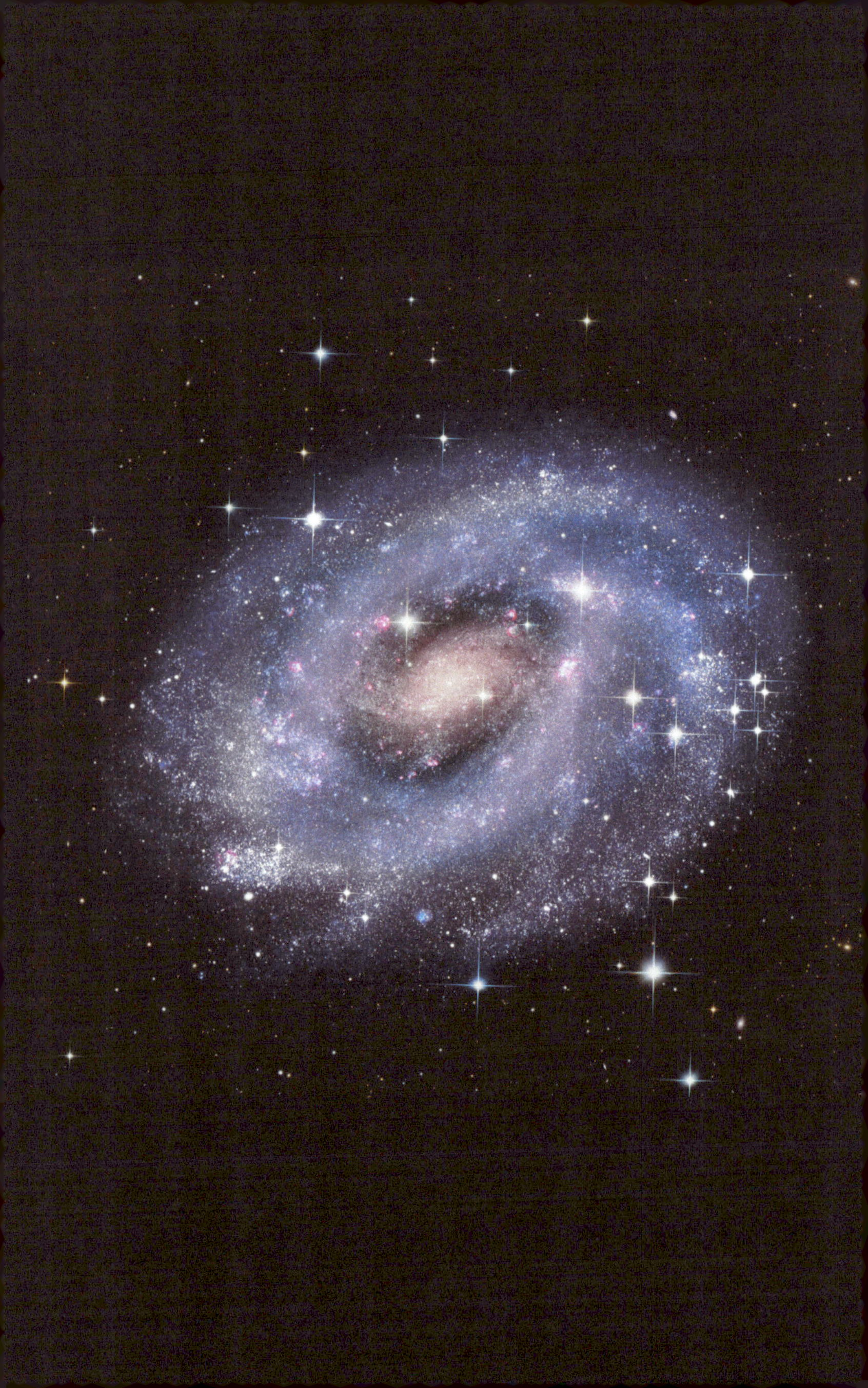

PART IV

Lanterns of Infinity

Faith, surrender, and the light that endures

NGC 300 is a pattern made visible, a soft spiral whose structure speaks long after its making. These poems follow that signal—listening for the mind inside motion, the presence carried through design.

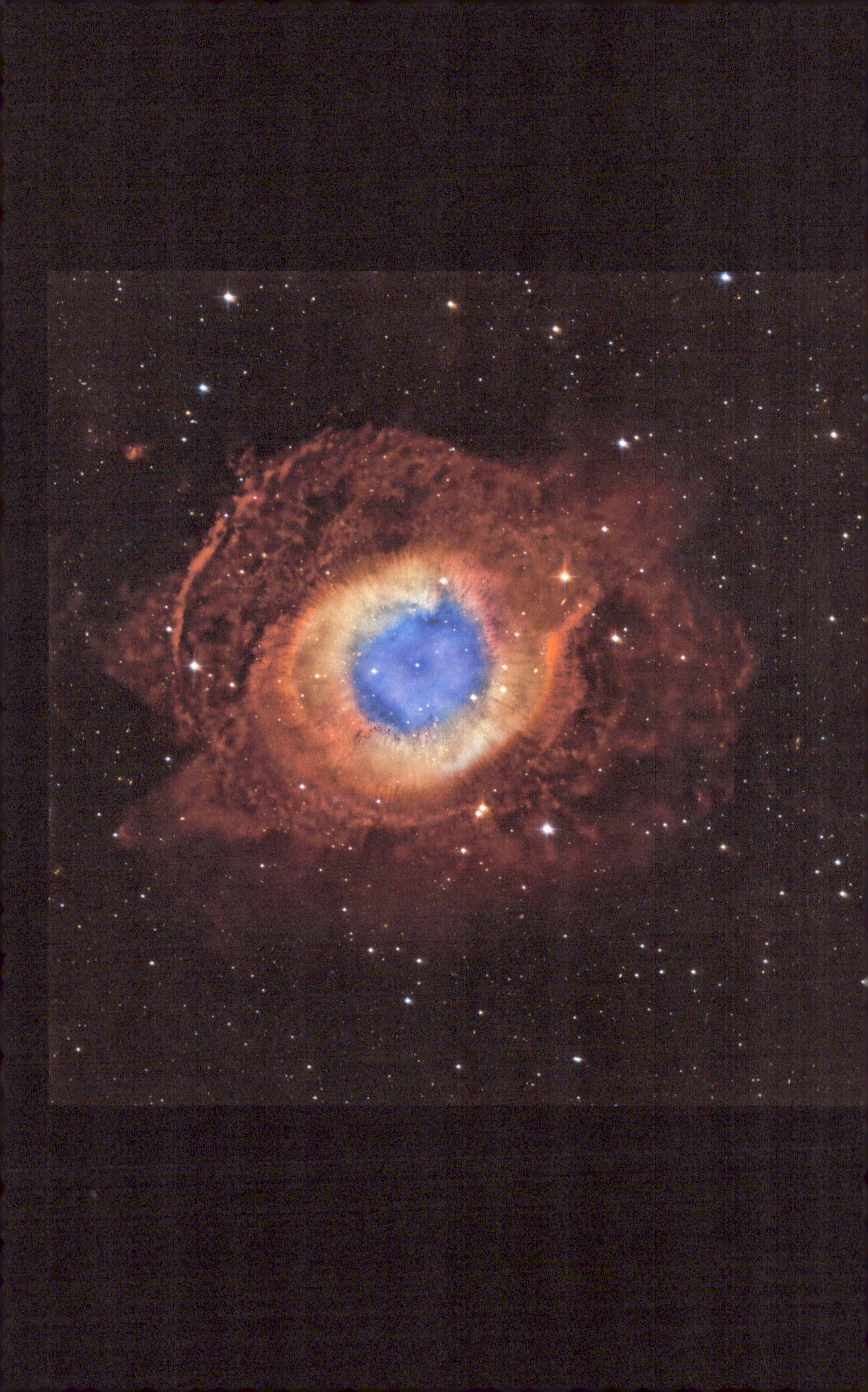

If We Must Speak of God

As a child, I was told to bow my head,
to sit still on hard pews
that left lines in the backs of my legs.

Prayer had a smell—
not bad,
but thick and unmistakable:
old paper, candle wax,
wool coats damp from rain.
It clung to me like smoke,
even after we left.

Prayer had a sound—
not the sermon itself,
but the quiet between phrases,
the coughs swallowed by sleeves,
the shuffling of fellow restless feet.

Prayer had a color—
a shifting haze
like dust caught in sunbeams,
gold one moment,
and gray the next,
depending on how the light fell
through the narrow stained glass windows.

Each week I was there,
while my friends were free.
Their voices floating on the wind,
sharing psalms of their own making.

My head swelled with
anger—
rebellion—
wishing I understood the rules
that seemed so obvious to others.
But the walls around their meaning
were too high for me to climb.
Confusion was my companion.

And yet, I cannot scorn the faithful.
I've seen shoulders unclench,
lips loosen in prayer,
grief easing,
bodies leaning
toward something I cannot touch.
From an oasis, they drink—
but I leave thirsty.
They walk with certainty;
I walk with questions.
I envy the warmth of their shelter.

So I found other sanctuaries.

At the ocean, the air smelled of salt and sun.
Gulls cried overhead like laughter,
a vendor's call—
Fudgy-wudgies! Ice cold fudgy-wudgies!—
mingling with the rhythm of the tide.

I stood at the edge
where the waves collapsed,
water rushing back to the sea,
sand washing away beneath my feet
until I felt I might vanish with it.
Children's castles crumbled beside me,
walls dissolving into mounds,
soon to disappear.
I learned impermanence there,
and humility—
how easily what we build
can be carried away.

The stars, sharp as frost,
watched without judgment,
their silence steadier
than any doctrine.
They required nothing—
no vows, no obedience—
only that I look up,
only that I listen.
And in their gaze,
I was small—
but not insignificant.

If we must speak of God,
let us first ask:
what do we mean?
A puppeteer?
A judge tallying sin?
Or a flicker behind the ribs,
a pull toward kindness,
a current binding us
when we treat each other as kin?
Not written in books,
but felt in the marrow.

And prayer—
let it be the salt wind
clinging to your skin
after patience steadies your hand;
the hush of laughter breaking silence
when forgiveness finds its way,
loosening your shoulders,
softening your jaw.
Let the light spill not through dust
but across every face,
warm as the morning sun on skin,
wide as the sky,
constant as the stars
falling on us all—
unconditional. Endless.

"If We Must Speak of God" considers religion — not the one inherited, but the one remade through living. The Helix Nebula, the remnant of a dying star, is often called the Eye of God, though what endures there is not sight but release: light carried outward from what is ending. The poem follows the same transformation. It leaves behind benches, sermons, and certainty to find holiness in motion — in the tide, in laughter, in patience, in the small flicker that stirs behind the ribs. Both image and text redefine worship as recognition: the divine not above us, but among us, continuous and human.

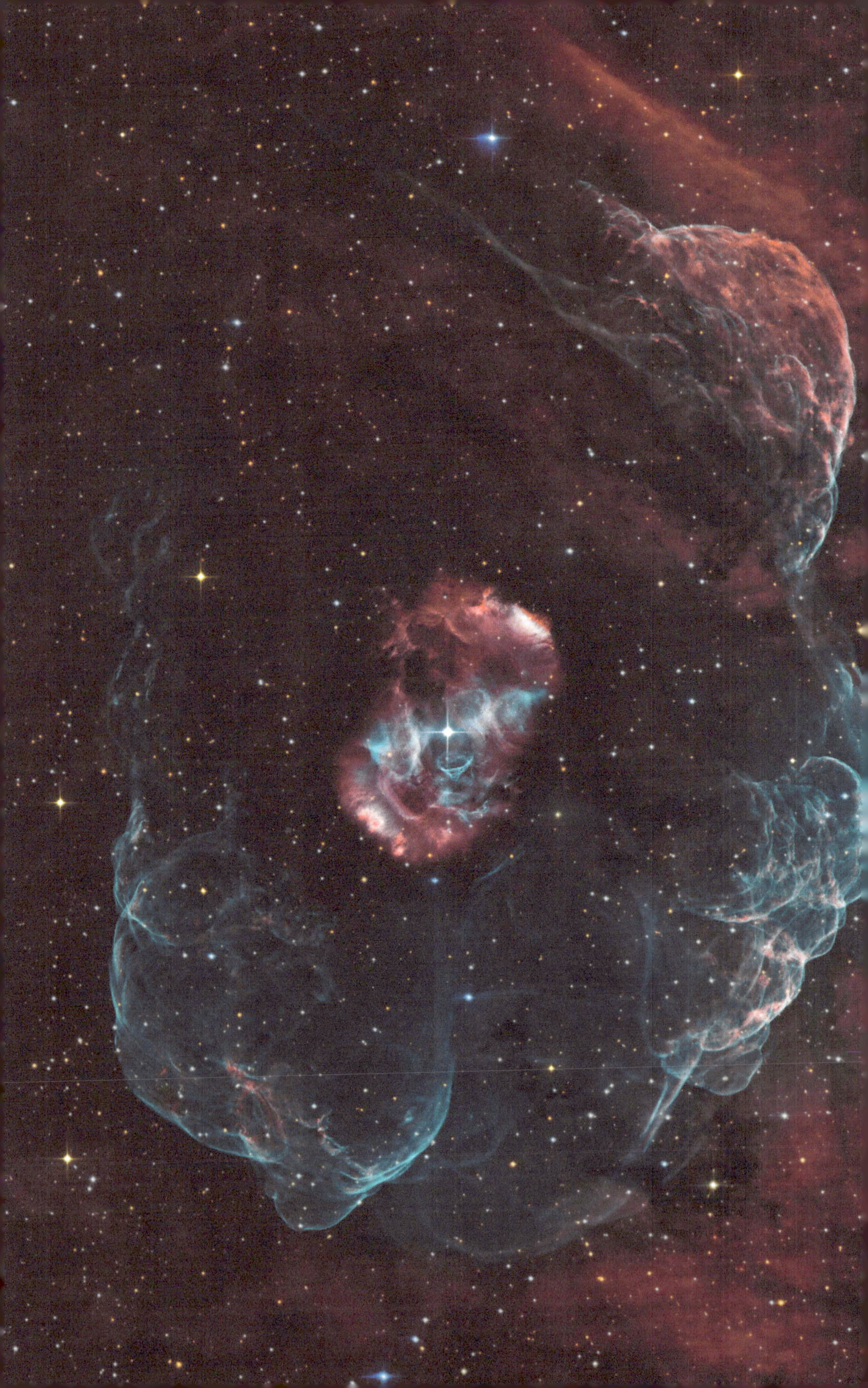

Stars in a Jar

She came in from the dark,
unbothered by it—
the kind of dark
you live with, not through.

A glass dome sat on the table,
not glowing,
but holding the memory of glow—
thin threads of elsewhere
wound into silence.

She asked,
not sharply, not dimly—
just with the uncreased voice
of someone who has never
needed the question:
"Do they speak?"

She meant the stars.
Or the jar.
Or perhaps the ones
who placed them there.

I might have answered
in the measure of orbits,
in the hum beneath silence.
Instead,
I said nothing,
and lifted the lid.

Out came no light,
only a hush that remembered light.

She blinked.

"But what does it feed?"
She meant the time,
the sleepless nights,
the turning of mirrors toward nothing.

I offered her the jar.
She held it—
felt the weight
of something not useful.
Not warm.
But awake.
As if a thousand hands had passed it down
and none had dropped it.

A kind of hush passed through her—
the pause between question
and the form it takes
when it learns to listen.

Later,
she would not recall what she saw.
Only that
some part of her joined the hush—
and in that stillness,
we rose a little higher.

"Stars in a Jar" is about knowledge — the kind built to be held, shared, and added to. The Dragon's Egg Nebula, NGC 6164, formed when a massive star expelled its outer layers, creating a luminous shell that contains what the star once was. It stands as a vessel for light, not a cage — a record of energy released to shape what follows. The poem sees knowledge the same way: a collective inheritance, each contribution joining the quiet body of understanding that lifts us all a little higher. Both image and text honor containment not as limitation, but as the structure that allows growth — a vessel built to pass light forward.

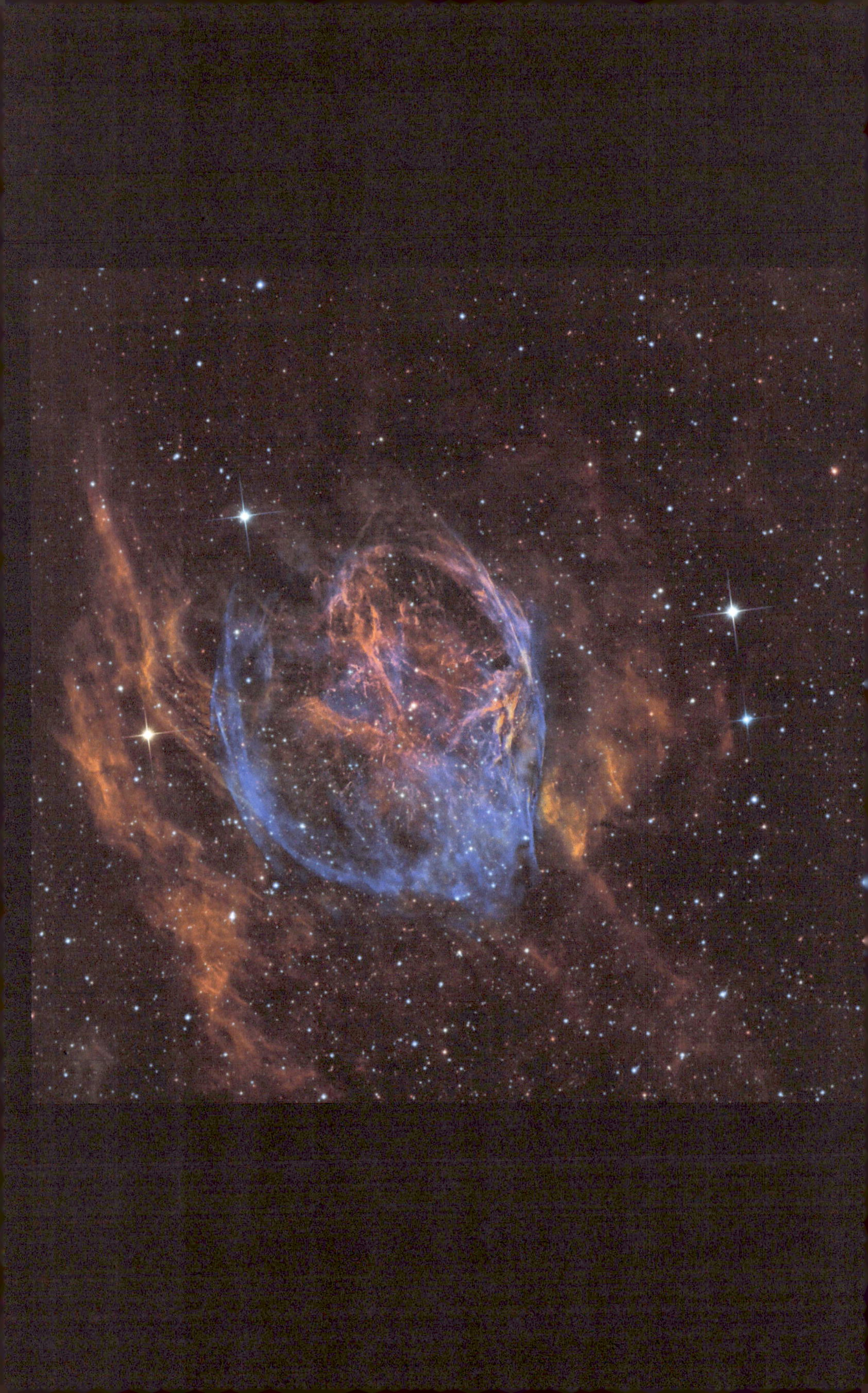

The Bubble

The black and silver bike,
the envy of his friends,
rested on its side in the driveway,
one wheel clicking its last few rotations.
The swing set—oversized, overbuilt—
stood in the corner like a silent kingdom
waiting for a ruler.

He ran past all of it.

Kneeling at the bowl of soap,
he dipped the wand, lifted it carefully—
a slow, deliberate breath,
as if he feared the magic might slip away.

The bubble rose.
At first, a faint shimmer.
Then—caught by the angle of the sun—
a rainbow gathered along its skin,
a thin trembling ring of color.

He chased it,
grass bending under his small steps,
shadow leaping beside him.
The bubble zigged upward,
dragging its soft rainbow behind it
like a kite made of light
tethered to his imagination.

As it floated higher,
the colors sharpened—
greens folding into blues,
reds flaring bright at the edges—
as though the rainbow knew
it was running out of surface to live on.

For a moment
the whole yard curved inside it:
the house,
the swing set,
his bright shirt,
a brief startled reflection—
all held in a globe no thicker than breath.

That was the peak:
the colors at their brightest,
the moment at its fullest,
the child reaching with both hands.

Then—
a shiver of light,
a sound softer than a silence shifting,
and the world pulled back into itself.

He stood still,
hand frozen midair,
the echo of color fading from his eyes.
The swing set behind him glinted.
A ball shadowed by a tree in the uncut grass
waited—
patient for what came next.

Nothing changed.
And yet everything felt a little sharper,
as if the bubble had left its brightness behind
in the things that remained.

RCW 104 is a wind-blown bubble—light stretched thin into a near-perfect sphere, its colors gathering along the rim where the structure is most fragile. What looks delicate is actually the record of motion: a breath of a star caught just before it dissipates.

The Bubble follows the same arc. A child's breath lifts a trembling ring of color that briefly holds the world inside it, then vanishes with a soft shiver of light. What lingers is not the bubble itself, but the brightness it leaves behind—sharpening everything that remains.

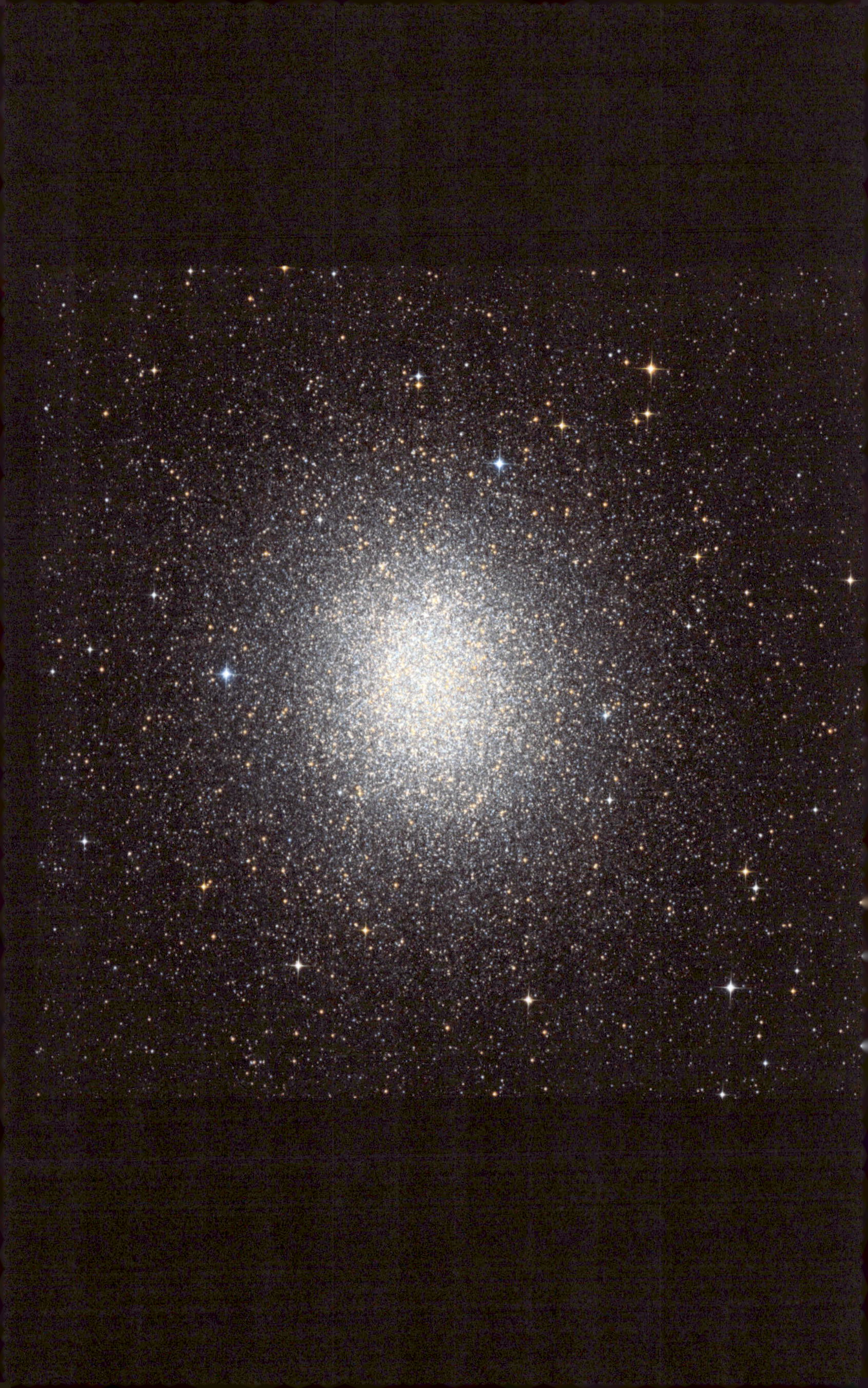

Open Hands

She believed the sky was meant to be entered,
not just looked at,
and that our dreams—
what we long for,
is already circling above us.

So I rose early,
stepping into the quiet of morning,
eyes following a bright-feathered bird—
the one I had carried inside me long before I saw it—
tracing the edge of the tree line.
I followed.

And I remembered being a child,
pointing a flashlight into the night,
reaching for something I could not name—
wondering if the beam ended
or simply went on forever.

Over the snag of roots,
through thorns that wrote stories on my arms.
Some days it vanished into glare.
Some days it sang
from beyond the ridge
where the path was only guesswork
and I walked by faith more than sight.

But by going,
the world unfolded:
crumbling stone walls leaning like thresholds
to futures I had only dared imagine,
a simple meal offered by someone
I hadn't known the day before,
a stream teaching me to wait
for the moment the surface clears.

Luck arrived like that—
quiet, earned—
the kind that finds those already moving.
I learned not to clutch at wings.
Open hands invite more than they seize.
So I stopped chasing.

I sat among tall reeds
and let the wind pass through me.

And one morning,
the bird returned—
light as a pulse—
settling on a branch near enough
that its trembling moved through my own chest.

I never closed my hand.

Omega Centauri is a dense cluster of stars held together by shared gravity. No single star controls the structure; the cluster forms because each one contributes to the whole. Its shape comes from many bodies moving together, not from anything grasped or claimed.

Open Hands reflects the same understanding.
The poem turns from chasing what is wanted to making space for what can arrive.
It recognizes that connection is not taken by force, but formed by presence, patience, and openness.

What stays is what is free to return.

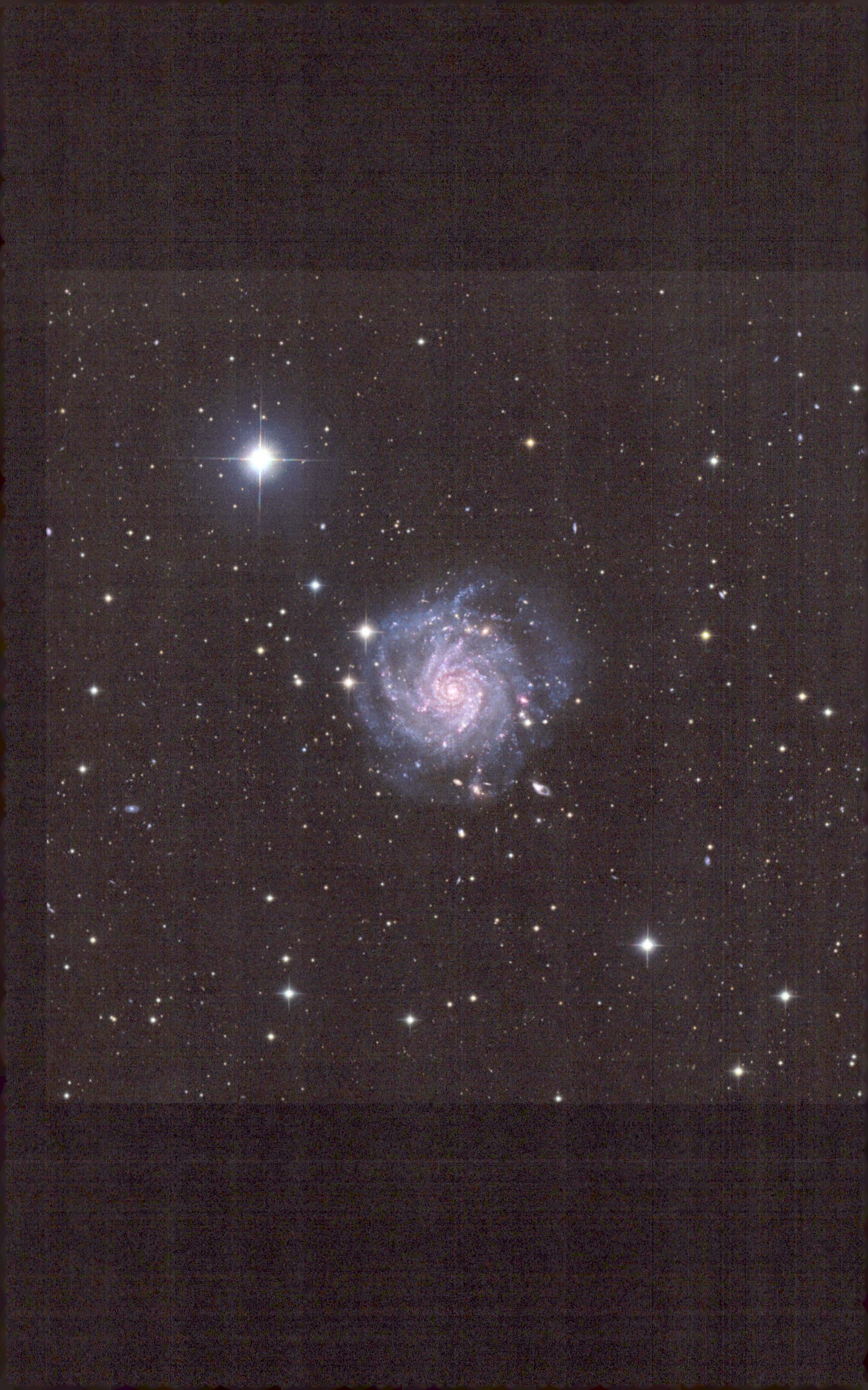

Coda
What Endures

What endures is not the flame,
but the warmth it leaves behind

IC 5332 is a spiral drawn in faint light, a structure that emerges only in stillness. The Coda rests in that same quiet—what remains after the voice falls away.

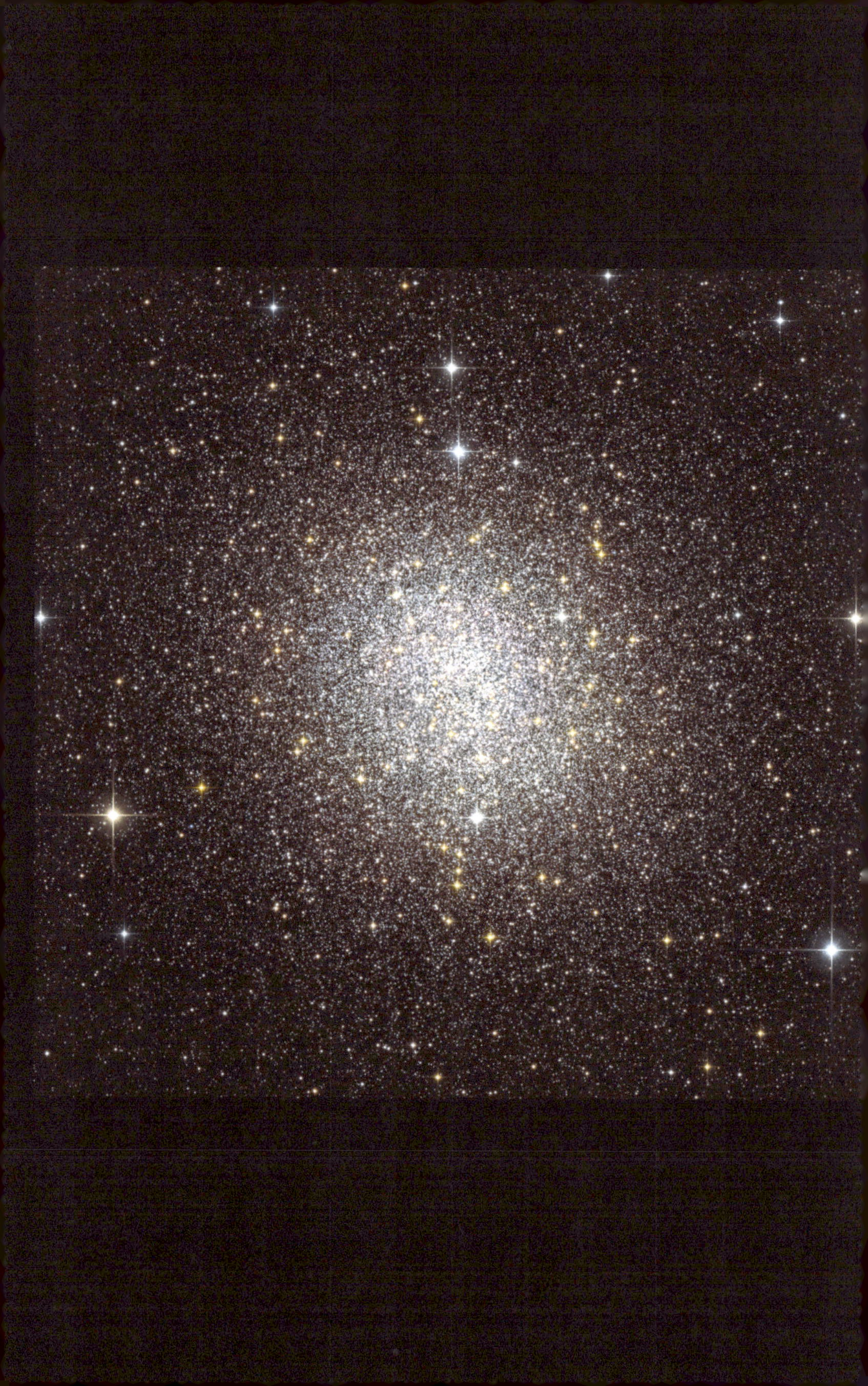

An Ember Passed On

I dreamt of a table—
three shadows leaning close,
voices stitched in care,
laughter weaving a net
to hold what age has frayed.

My granddaughters were older then.
Even from that distance,
I felt the subtle strength of love.

And yet, for now,
I wonder what ember I'm leaving behind—
a hush of stories,
burning in their becoming?
Or a flicker too faint
to guide them?

Now they sleep in quilts beside me
while I read them books,
my voice wandering
into their earliest dreams.

Morning comes, wide-eyed—
three faces hide in the doorway,
awaiting a surprise.

A breakfast is pulled
from memory and invention,
plates warm with secrets
only grandparents keep.

One spills their milk,
another negotiates for "just one more pancake,"
the third sings a song with the wrong words, proudly,
and somehow it's perfect.

And still—
preparing for the day—
I send a wish ahead
that they keep a thirst for wonder,
so when the music calls,
they do not turn away.

Sometimes,
when the quiet settles,
an arm loops around my neck—
not careful, just certain—
an unexpected snuggle
that folds the years into minutes.

I keep the lantern lit,
knowing dawn will widen past my arms.
Still, I hope its glow
marks the sky enough
to guide them,
to carry them forward
beyond what once kept the dark at bay.

Every lantern dreams
of the day its light goes on
without it.

And when they return,
as they often do,
we gather at that same table—
edges worn smooth with years,
our laughter mending
what time unmade.

There, in the lull between stories,
I see the ember glowing—
not in my keeping,
but in theirs.

An Ember Passed On" turns on generations — what endures because it's carried forward. 47 Tucanae, a cluster of some of the oldest stars in the Milky Way, still shines with the light of beginnings billions of years old. The poem speaks of human inheritance in the same way: the warmth of work, care, and memory passed from generation to generation, each tending what was left to them. Both image and text see continuity not as repetition but renewal — an ember kept alive by many hands, its glow unchanged even as the keepers change.

Afterward

A telescope gathers light;
a poem gathers silence.
Both reach toward what cannot be held,
and both return changed.

— Aphelion

Daniel Stern is a retired engineer turned astronomer/astrophotographer. His poetry explores the intersection of grief, silence, and renewal—where language becomes both vessel and bridge. *Aphelion*, his debut collection of poems and astrophotographs, traces the distances love must travel and the light that endures across them.

The book is dedicated to his son, Mitchell—"whose absence became the spark, whose silence taught me to speak"—a guiding presence throughout his creative journey. He lives in Delray Beach, Florida, with his wife, Randie.

www.ingramcontent.com/pod-product-compliance
Lightning Source LLC
LaVergne TN
LVHW052253100826
845147LV00001B/30

* 9 7 9 8 9 9 4 0 3 8 4 0 6 *